Between Two Enlightenments

This edition first published in hardback in Great Britain in
2021 by Maclean Dubois
14/2 Gloucester Place, Edinburgh EH3 6EF

ISBN: 978-0-9565278-9-9

Copyright © Lance St John Butler, 2021

All rights reserved. No part of this publication may
be reproduced, stored, or transmitted in any form, or
by any means electronic, mechanical or photocopying,
recording or otherwise, without the express written
permission of the publisher.

The moral right of Lance St John Butler to be identified as the
author of this work has been asserted by him in accordance with
the Copyright, Designs and Patents Act 1988.

British Library Cataloguing-in-Publication Data
A catalogue record for this book is available on request
from the British Library.

Designed and typeset by Abigail Salvesen.
Printed and bound by Gutenberg Press Ltd, Malta.

Between Two Enlightenments

Chaumer Essays

LANCE ST JOHN BUTLER

Maclean Dubois

CONTENTS

1. Two?	7
2. Why the Enlightenment?	12
3. Me too? The Last Gasp of an Older World	26
4. 'Je suis Charlie'	38
5. The Importance of History	46
6. Proust's Way	57
7. Subjective and Experiential, or Objective and Experimental?	74
8. Happiness	81
9. The Priesthood of Science	88
10. 'And is that all?'	96
11. The Religion of Social Justice	102
12. Consciousness is Enlightenment	113

Note

In early 2020 The Chaumer café on Queen Street in Edinburgh set up a series of lectures to be held on the last Thursday evening of each month, we hoped for years to come. The topic was to be the Enlightenment, partly in honour of the Georgian splendour of the New Town by which the café is surrounded.

The first two evenings, in January and February that year, went well and the third was being anticipated with pleasure when Britain was assaulted by the coronavirus pandemic and then locked down on 23 March.

During the ensuing hiatus in normal life I felt it appropriate to write down some thoughts about the Enlightenment, a subject which I had been obliged to consider more clearly than ever before by the exigencies of lecturing to a discerning audience.

What follows in this volume is the result of that opportunity, created by enforced idleness.

1. Two?

When in 1784 Kant noticed some intellectual changes around him and saw that Europe was moving towards a more rational form of thinking he published an essay with a rather surprising title: *Beantwortung der Frage: Was ist Aufklärung?* In English, 'Answering the Question: What is Enlightenment?'

This title proclaims a dialogue, an ongoing argument, apparently between Kant and the coiner of this new term but in fact between the new age and the old one. The essay begins: 'Enlightenment is man's emergence from his self-incurred immaturity.' That last word (*Unmündigkeit* in German) also translates as 'childishness' or even 'impudence' and literally means 'un-mouthedness', which more or less equates it to the English word 'infancy' whose etymology reveals the meaning 'unable to speak', though you could be forgiven for not knowing this if you go past an infants' school at playtime. In other words Kant sees enlightenment as a move from babbling to serious talk.

Aufklärung also has connotations of 'clearing up' in both the meteorological and 'tidy-your-room' senses. The Enlightenment was clearing away the rubbish of earlier centuries, for instance such things as superstition, magic and autocracy, and bringing some light into the now-tidy room so that proper thinking could occur. The French expression for this process, and for the eighteenth century in general, is '*Les Lumières*', which evokes the switching on of multiple lights; Spanish has '*La Iluminación*'.

But since Eastern religion began to make an impact on the West in the nineteenth century we have also tended to use the e-word to refer to the Buddhist experience of a new spiritual vision. The key similarity between the Rationalist and Buddhist versions of E/enlightenment lies in their ambition to *see clearly* what has happened and is happening to humanity and to remove obfuscations and illusions. The e-word has consequently come to be used in connection with two opposed forces in modern culture: Rationalism and Buddhism. Kant wants us to grow up and see more clearly.

The Buddha's version, as in 'and it was then that he was enlightened', could be reworded as something like 'and then he *saw the big picture*'.

Behind this dichotomy lies a deeper rift, the one supposed to exist between science on the one hand and religion or spirituality on the other. I am certainly not the only person to have found myself caught in the intellectual landfill between these two groups of ideas, but now I suggest that we can see their relationship more clearly: there is room for negotiation here and we may find that each side, appropriately enough, *illuminates* the other. The evolutionary psychologist and writer on meditation Robert Wright tells us that

> Enlightenment in the Buddhist sense has something in common with enlightenment in the Western scientific sense: it involves becoming more aware of what causes what. (*Why Buddhism is True*, 2018)

The essays that follow move from one of these forms of enlightened thinking to the other via some deviations and consider their common goal of greater and clearer awareness of what is going on. They suggest that we need both kinds of clear thinking. But the Buddhist version is the more urgent need today.

There is an overall thesis here. It is that the eighteenth-century Enlightenment gave us an immense gift which we have not rejected or taken back or exchanged for anything else. This gift, however, is not without its dangers and it doesn't provide an explanation for everything that we know or experience. To get nearer to the bigger picture we need something like the best thinking of the Buddha, or at least something that will bring us closer to our own experiences than rational analysis alone can. Perhaps we can manage a marriage between these two enlightenments?

We are in an unusual intellectual place. Douglas Murray is one of the few voices who has dared ask whether we haven't, like Othello, thrown away a pearl richer than all our tribe. In *The Strange Death of Europe* (2018) and *The Madness of Crowds* (2019) he argues that the cradle of the Enlightenment and all it stands for (Europe of course) is in danger of sinking not only under a tidal wave of migration from places where Enlightenment values are, to say the least, disregarded, but more deeply in danger of losing its self-confidence as the world's first Enlightened culture. We now prefer to apologise for being European, regret most of our past and many of our real liberal values and give preference instead to often-violently-expressed politically-correct obsessions with race, gender and class. For the modern 'woke' indignant not much that white people have done now really counts against the stain of slavery (though

Shakespeare, Newton and Darwin were members of that group), nothing that men have done really counts against the oppression of women (though among the many men we would now call sexist we can count, for instance, Milton, Hegel and Gandhi) and anything that smacks of privilege cannot count against the oppression of the unprivileged (though 'the privileged' must include Socrates, Montaigne and Wittgenstein).

Exacerbating this lack of self-confidence that we feel in the things that Europe invented (things that the world has largely adopted) is the current all-conquering globalisation, a movement which has good and bad sides. Dealing with everyone from everywhere is a recipe for reducing bad differences such as pointless preconceptions about race, but it is also a recipe for ignoring differences found in countries with other cultural norms. Things which should be 'universal', like freedom from tyranny and torture, stand a better chance of becoming more widespread as we trade and communicate with each other more, and that can only be good; but the concomitant and contradictory idea that all cultures are equally valid, promoted by our desire to respect those others with whom we are now in closer contact, can encourage us to turn a blind eye to the fact that these new and closer neighbours may have cultural norms that should be called out.

By way of example: when feminist intellectuals have been questioned about other countries they have been known to try to defend Female Genital Mutilation on the grounds that we shouldn't interfere with the way things are done elsewhere. Paid-up left-liberals defend the veiling of women and criticise the Somali-American heroine Ayaan Hirsi Ali who escaped a Koran-only education, beatings and a forced marriage at age 15 to become a Dutch MP and a Harvard professor only to find once in the West that her exposure of these Islamic methods is regarded as a politically-incorrect gesture that does not respect a foreign culture. Her books are now on an official list of 'Islamophobic' publications. The liberations of enlightened thinking seem to have gone into a weird reverse and ended up with us ignoring the plight of tortured women and trying to ban their books.

What we need from the two enlightenments now is a certain detachment. Looking over the head of the bitter anger that fills the new social media, and is not absent from the old, we need to remember how we got here and on whose shoulders. The European Enlightenment led us to this point, but its aim was to liberate us, not to forge new manacles for our minds. We saw that fact clearly enough when we overthrew the pseudo-rational regime of the gulags and the Berlin Wall fell, but the West has now lurched into a place of un-self-confidence, self-dislike and mutual hatred that would have alarmed Locke or Voltaire or Kant.

Equally we need some detachment from the materialism (in both its senses) that was the unintended consequence of the Enlightenment. The path to that detachment may lead to a better understanding that the universe is not made of matter only, indeed may not exist in any very solid state at all and may itself depend on consciousness. This is the path allegedly first perceived under an Indian tree on 15 April 589 BC. The lesson of the Buddha is as important in our post-Enlightenment world as it has ever been.

2. Why the Enlightenment?

It's not just that Enlightenment thinking with a capital E is *better* than other kinds of thinking; modern thinking *is* Enlightenment thinking. Other kinds of mental activity are fine in their way and no doubt have their uses as we shall see, but they aren't really *thinking*. We are wedded to, and indeed our minds are now largely made of, patterns of thought of a specific kind; for us real thinking is evidential, logical, rational, proportionate and falsifiable. We live in the Hermeneutic Circle: theory gives way to new evidence and new evidence is approached logically and rationally before being modified into an improved theory. This is the only way that thinking is now able to be done.

The classic examples are well known. Galileo, following Copernicus, found evidence that the 'fixed stars' moved and was thus able to demonstrate the probability that the Ptolemaic theory of the universe would have to be revised. Darwin found evidence that species had changed over time and was thus able to develop the theory of evolution to replace the biblical account. Since Galileo and Darwin quite a lot has changed in cosmology and biology (so their work was falsifiable and not immutable) but the paradigms they proposed are still with us.

Einstein worked the other way round and suggested theoretical equations to explain how the forces of the universe should work; the evidence produced since his time has confirmed the accuracy of his theory though quantum physics has modified and is even in conflict to some extent with his ideas. With Einstein the Newtonian paradigm was found to be 'false' in that it wasn't a total explanation, though it has remained useful for everyday life. We all know how these things play out, how some thoughts cannot now be taken seriously and how the protocols of research and deduction follow known patterns. This is Enlightenment thinking.

Another example is readily available in the field of parapsychology. Here we make all sorts of assumptions that can appear illogical or unproven. Researchers delve into telepathy, channelling, precognition, psychokinesis and other paranormal events, all the things that are taken seriously by those interested in a non-materialist approach to unexplained phenomena. Such investigators may wish they could rely on a different kind of thinking, one which would be more appropriate to this field where normal explanations are often unavailable and where it is hard to replicate and to test. How, after all, could one apply normal rational thinking to a convincing Near-Death Experience account or to the apparition of a convincing ghost? 'Psi' phenomena such as these, and such as poltergeists and channelling, could perhaps be real, and some of them are certainly well-attested, but it is noticeable that when investigators try to explain them they don't use a non-rational or paranormal method; they are unlikely to claim '*I'm tuning in to a psychic vibration*' as a convincing argument against scepticism, and they are unlikely to say they are going to use some new way of explaining their thoughts; on the contrary they apply the most ordinary logical and scientific tests.[1] They seek evidence and corroboration, they look for alternative explanations, they speculate and measure, and they take the phenomena, where possible, into the laboratory. There isn't another, different, viable, 'spiritual' or 'paranormal' way of thinking about even these things. There is only one way of thinking.

Similarly, in the outer reaches of quantum mechanics, where we are in the presence of things that even Einstein balked at, we don't find scientists giving up on the rational and setting off to find a new way of thinking; all their protocols of normal logic remain in place even when they are confronted by such puzzles as wave-particle ambiguity or Einstein's 'spooky action at a distance', his comment on the observable behaviour of particles as they influence each other instantaneously however widely separated. These phenomena are rather like parapsychological effects as it happens, telepathy being spooky action at a distance too. And they too are analysed, as far as possible, with the usual Enlightenment tools.

The rational norms with which we now think can also be found in the humanities: eighteenth-century texts such as Gibbon's *Decline and Fall* are models of historiography because, unsurprisingly, history as a proper discipline first saw serious light in the Age of Reason. And why then? Because objective, logical and evidence-based history,

---

1 Ramon Llull, the medieval polymath and perhaps the first modern novelist (*Blanquerna*, 1283) wrote, as one of a series of poetic stanzas, '*The bird was singing in the garden of the Beloved. The Lover came and said to the bird: - If we don't understand each other through language, let's communicate through love, because your song represents my Beloved to my eyes.*' But no examples of the way this communication was effected are given.

history based on research, didn't exist before the Enlightenment. Thucydides, known as 'the father of scientific history', is a famous partial exception with the fixation on facts in his *History of the Peloponnesian War* (fifth century BC); but more representative are Herodotus, Froissart or Geoffrey of Monmouth who can only be called historians because there isn't anything else to call them but who were quite undeterred by lack of evidence, unashamed of making things up and happy to contradict themselves. That was normal both in the ancient world and in the medieval world, but come the Renaissance and *a fortiori* come the eighteenth century all such history writing is quietly consigned to the cabinet of curiosities as being quaint, unreliable and at best indicative of a particular mindset, but no more. Then, with the Enlightenment, history-writing begins to operate on the basis we have used ever since, and here again it is evidence, logic, reason and provisional theory that rule the day.

Thinking remains Enlightenment thinking even when we are puzzled and appear to have hit a contradiction. It is *always the same* however much we find new anomalous elements in the universe or paranormal events in our own experience. The notion of the Mystery is overdone. That black holes do things that we struggle to understand fully, or that some Precognition experiments produce 'impossible' positive results, or indeed that Dogs Know When Their Owners Are Coming Home (which it seems they magically do – I'm quoting the title of one of Rupert Sheldrake's books) doesn't mean that we have to abandon our rational principles; on the contrary, we keep calm and carry on with our usual measuring and collecting of evidence, and we work on a new theory that we hope will accommodate these recalcitrant things. There's no alternative.

But we should avoid the trap known as promissory materialism. This is the lazy assumption, made by scientism, that even if there are things we don't understand now *one day* everything will be explained just as it is now, that is according to the present materialist paradigm. However, *au contraire*, the very essence of modern science and of Enlightenment thinking, from its origins with Francis Bacon up until today, is that it is an *exploration* that is never finished. The present paradigm will no more be the last than Newton's was, solid as it seemed for two hundred years. The duty of the rationalist is to find new adaptations, to make new arrangements of the evidence, to allow new evidence into the fold once it has been seen to have some credibility, to *try things out*. And that, very precisely, is what the Enlightenment taught us and the method that the eighteenth century came up with which, contrary to a scientific belief in fixedness, is a method absolutely flexible and infinitely open to rearrangement. The only limitation to this is that, although paradigms can and will change, real thinking, even with its open-minded willingness to alter a view and to rearrange ideas, will always have to remain as far as possible logical, rational and based on the evidence.

Promissory materialists and scientists who will brook no opposition to the present paradigm may look like Enlightenment thinkers but they aren't. Their methods are reasonable and thus unexceptionable, but only up to the point where they claim certainty; at that point, where they reach absolute unquestioning adherence to an exclusive materialist (or any other) theory without any court of appeal, they flip over and become unscientific and thus betray the intellectual ethics of the Enlightenment.

So it is not that the *contents* of modern thought are all solid rock, on the contrary they change all the time, it is rather that the *methods* of the Enlightenment are the only ones that will do the job we call thinking. Even under the onslaught of the poststructuralist and deconstructive ideas that have beset the modern mind since the 1960s the Enlightenment method remains firm. We take rational attitudes towards deconstructive propositions just as we do to the inexplicable propositions of quantum mechanics or parapsychology, and if we find them irrational then we look again at our theoretical framework or our evidence or both rather than abandoning our method in favour of another.

One of the first subjects to undergo poststructuralist reformation in the universities of the 1970s and 1980s was the study of literature. Here for instance one of the fruitful slogans of the new thinking was that 'a text declares one thing but demonstrates another'. Thus a text 'deconstructs itself' and the business of the critic is to show how this works. Much excitement was engendered by this at the theoretical level for here, surely, was a big new job for the critic and the literature professor: now more or less equal to the original writer, he or she could show how texts don't mean what they say and show that meaning is, more generally, radically elusive in a way that can be spun out *ad inifinitum* – a great boon for critics and teachers working on writers about whom previously it had been thought that perhaps everything had already been said. This was not at all a bad starting point for a new relativist intellectual world order in which opinion has tended to trump truth as the ultimate criterion of sense and it shook things up; but it did not dislodge the primacy of the Enlightenment method.

For behold! The critic and the professor, faced with these smart new ideas full of deliberate self-contradiction and a refusal to recognise 'truths', *in reality* went about deconstructing most normally and rationally. What was declared in the text (say, the desirability of a quasi-emasculated patriarchy in *Jane Eyre*) was undermined by a counter-tendency in Brontë's novel that demonstrates that Jane is the most competent and effective actor in the novel, a point possibly backed up by the fact that the sham masculine pseudonym of the author, 'Currer Bell', concealed a real woman. But this reading-with-contradictions, sometimes interestingly called 'symptomatic reading', was, like any other interpretation, argued through evidence, through close attention to the text, through common sense, through rational proposals and a testing of those proposals, through historical research, linguistic pointers, bibliographical scholarship, etymological analysis and all the rest. In fact the full panoply of academic tools was deployed in the usual way, and academic tools provide, of course, the only way of thinking in universities, and universities are centrally and exclusively the children of the Enlightenment. There is no escape.

And Heaven help the undergraduate whose literature essay, attempting to emulate the spirit of the poststructuralist times, reads like Derrida at his most playful (and opaque) or like Lacan at any time. No good grade will come from a purely-relativist piece of work. It's hard even to know what such a thing would be, but if it existed it would fail – fail not only in the university grading system but also fail to convey anything other than a vague shadow of . . . of whatever it is that the student . . . errm . . . is or isn't *really* writing about (except there can be no 'really'.)

At the professorial level too things look very odd. There are one or two good books on Derrida which explain his thinking in clear, logical, rational terms – which from our point of view should be unsurprising because 'Whatever can be said can be said clearly' as Wittgenstein told us – but there are also handbooks devoted to Derrida's work that have lamentably taken the full deconstructive shilling without adhering to rational norms. In these you will find chapters called 'Introduction' which are nothing more than an attack on *the notion of an introduction*, and chapters purporting to tell of the great philosopher's life that contain *no biographical information at all* because that would be too definite and politically-loaded a piece of knowledge. Such books are gobbledegook and a cheat. What after all has the reader who paid his or her £9.99 to obtain 'a book on Derrida' or 'something about deconstruction' parted with his or her money *for*?

But we need a warning here. For although Enlightenment thought is inescapably the stuff of all modern thought, its methods can be used to good or bad ends. Logical thinking is a species of machine which does not itself have any prejudices or any interest in these 'goods' and 'bads' and is thus limited in one way. A simple example can be found in the contested area of education. Here the method of rational thinking is ubiquitous, the Enlightenment project is in full swing and we mostly approve of schools and universities. Nonetheless, we might ask, what should the school curriculum consist of?

The decision to include one thing and not another in a curriculum is not really the business of enlightened thinking beyond the basic idea that it is clearly intolerable and self-contradictory to teach unanalysed, non-enlightened ideas as truth or to invent pieces of fake knowledge. It cannot be acceptable, for instance, to teach as 'truth' the tenets of religions that have been exploded by reason: there seems to be inadequate evidence that Jesus was born of a virgin, for instance, so that is a claim that cannot be taught unquestioned in any respectable academic environment. And one might well question, and therefore leave out of the curriculum, the appearance of the Angel Gabriel to the prophet Mohammed – or indeed the very existence of an entity called 'the Angel Gabriel'.

There are, however, perfectly respectable rational claims that can be made by the branch of sociology or psychology we now call 'religious studies' (rather than 'theology' or 'divinity'). It is a historical, sociological and psychological fact that large populations have believed in the Virgin Birth, and a fact that that belief has an anthropological history that can be traced through literature and art for instance; it is a topic that can be studied and analysed like any other. The Angel Gabriel has a part to play in the history of several religions. Even the students studying in what were departments of divinity in the older universities are no longer expected to be paid-up believers as they were when Oxford and Edinburgh were the main training establishments for Anglican and Kirk clergy. Now, post-Enlightenment, they are much more likely to be studying new-age religions or the sociology of some sect. Enlightenment thinking has overtaken belief as the way we proceed intellectually, and it has swept the board.

But it is only a method and it may conceal other problems. Look for instance at our 'religious studies' departments which apply this method to what was once 'divinity'. The new method is comparative, historical, analytical and open-minded, but then we hit another checkpoint: for although objective truth is the goal of history, sociology and psychology they are *themselves* contentious subjects. How much Marx is being used in the course or in our research for instance? How much Freud? How many of the principles of Durkheim or Jung still apply? What emphasis is put on the economy, or on the women, of the period in question? Should that matter? What statistical methods are being employed? What conceptual frameworks? And so on. The *method* remains the same: evidence, reason and logic are the watchwords. But since we cannot do everything, and in most education we can only do very little, what should we teach or bother to research into? Choices of what to do with science are not scientific choices, as is well known. The limits of the Enlightenment are to be found at the gates of academia, outside those humanity may do its worst, or its best, as it sees fit.

And it does. At the *best* end there are the extraordinary discoveries of science, the amazing new abilities given to humankind: flying to the moon, talking to relatives in Australia without leaving Dundee, lives being prolonged by incredible medicines and so on. But at the *worst* end we can remember that monsters such as Pol Pot had Parisian educations and worked out logically that the best thing to do with the weapons made possible by Enlightenment science was to kill everybody. Then there were the town planners who destroyed some of the best parts of our cities and replaced them with motorways or gimcrack soulless towers where human beings were dumped and allowed to descend into lives of despairing, violent, drug-addicted criminality without any hope or wider vision. These were disasters that followed in the wake of thinking that seemed, how shall we put it? . . . *to be right at the time*. The analysis and the statistics pushed politicians and planners one way – reason had to prevail! But the results were catastrophic.

It goes further than this too. For some of the best things that Enlightenment thinking is ultimately responsible for are, paradoxically, actually and truly killing us. Why, for instance, is there overpopulation and starvation on our rich planet if not because medical and public health advances made since the mid-nineteenth century, and the work of charities such as Oxfam, have produced a population explosion? Why is there global warming if not because of the invention of the internal combustion and jet engines? Why can we now wipe out our species at the touch of few buttons? Science and reason may have doomed us to extinction.

And yet the great method still works for all that. After all, it may be rational in our circumstances to *ration* things, and perhaps a distribution of everything on a better basis might in the end mean fewer mouths to feed (it is the poor who have the babies). Surely it would now be rational to bring most travelling by aeroplane to an end. It is rational, because healthier, to walk rather than take the car. *De facto*, reason may turn out not to be a machine that is entirely neutral as far as consequences go – it would be irrational for instance for it not to support certain values which, although complicated at the detail or political level, are surely easy to agree at the global. Avoiding certain obvious catastrophes, for instance, may be the only way to keep *homo sapiens* from disappearing, and if the species vanishes human reason itself will vanish too.

It is thus illogical to exclude value from *all* discussion of Enlightenment thinking; but it is right that we cannot let it have the last word. If the *first* word, which is the advancement of knowledge driven by the universities, laboratories, think-tanks, big tech companies, the internet and all the other products of the Enlightenment means that we can now communicate almost instantaneously all round the globe, for instance, it doesn't follow that everyone should do this all the time, or conversely be forbidden from doing it. The last word, or at least a later word, might well be to consider whether such communication is dangerous for the health of children addicted to their mobile phones and other devices or whether it is 'good for society'. Second thoughts might also find that some idea of 'real' communication is at risk if we do all our interactions in cyberspace. These are not really questions for scientists and need to be discussed in other forums.

Enlightenment thinkers seem to have felt that there was a fairly straightforward way into the future through education, reform and rational planning. Light would dawn, they felt, more or less of itself as these areas were worked on. But in reality they couldn't see into the future very clearly and the main value of their thinking was surely that they helped to get rid of some of the tenebrous qualities of the past. The French Revolution, that most rationalist of endeavours, is a good example. Nobody could deny that the *ancien régime* had many dark corners that needed to be revealed, removed and replaced, that someone had to undertake the clearing away of rubbish. Looking back it was easy to see the rubbish for what it was – but looking *forward* was murkier, and the horrors of the September massacres of 1792, of the Terror, and of the near-genocide of the Vendée were quickly to demonstrate how hard that second stage of any improvement could be. And then the 'rational society' itself, also known as 'the Enlightenment Project', developed into the abysmal Soviet Union. One might say that it lasted, in practice, for almost exactly two hundred years from 14 July 1789 to 9 November 1989 when the Berlin Wall fell.

The Enlightenment is associated with socialism because state control seemed to the enlightened minority in the eighteenth century to be the only possible direction to take; it was a new future-orientated road, and socialism was in strong contrast to what had gone before throughout history (except for its tendency to authoritarianism). But what did it turn out to be in practice? It is hard to have much enthusiasm for Franco but one must face the fact that on the 'enlightened' socialist side of the Spanish Civil War in the 1930s a reasoned argument was made in favour of the killing of priests, and in the same decade the starving to death of seven million Kulaks and others by communist forces in Russia and the Ukraine was justified by rational commissars. These massacres were an effort to rid the world of pernicious elements that were holding back what was thought of as human progress. But, as these examples show, something went wrong between the theory and the practice.

Our Enlightenment thinking permits things both bad and good then. One can perhaps strike a balance between the good ideas and the horrors: if the Killing Fields were the result of Pol Pot's Marxist education in Paris, it was Marx's predecessors the French *philosophes* who had begun the work that would lead to our notions of human rights and the rule of law.

The Enlightenment was a once-off awakening which, whether we see the results as having been better or worse, we cannot undo. The only question is what to think in the world it has produced. For we are not going to fall silent even if there really is 'only one way of thinking now'. Not all conclusions are obvious, as we shall see, and we certainly need *something else*, as well as Enlightenment thinking, in the twenty-first century.[2]

---

2 One of Philip Goff's excellent books on panpsychism is called *Galileo's Error*. This title refers to the fact that Galileo, like Bacon and all their successors, chose to define material reality as that which can be measured; mathematics thus became the gold standard of scientific and subsequently Enlightenment thinking. But, as Goff points out, wonderfully successful though this choice has been in terms of science, it was an 'error' insofar as it explicitly left untouched a number of unmathematisable aspects of the universe, notably consciousness and the subjective, not to mention the paranormal and the spiritual.

3. Me Too? The Last Gasp of an Older World

Western history is conventionally divided into the Classical, the Medieval and the Modern. Modern history is subdivided into the Early Modern (1500–1700) and the Modern *tout court* (1700 to the present). Peter Laslett's brilliant study *The World We Have Lost* of 1965 chooses the date 1750 as being the last moment at which the old world was still intact. He gives dozens of examples in a cogent argument, but for now I will restrict myself to borrowing just one. It is that the combined armies that fought at the Battle of Naseby in 1645 numbered 29,000 men *in toto*, and this is thought to have been the largest grouping of humans in Britain that had ever occurred. In contrast a big rugby match today can attract 80,000 spectators at Twickenham or 60,000 at Murrayfield. You can leave alone all the inventions of modernity from the steam engine to space travel – the post-Enlightenment world has even invented *crowds*. Ignore for a moment the historical uniqueness of women wearing trousers or having a political say – there are probably more women (let alone people) in one place on any day at Wimbledon each year than were ever gathered together anywhere before 1750.

There was once an older, smaller world, then, and we have 'lost' it with extraordinary completeness since 1750, and lost it largely because of the overwhelming influence and efficiency of Enlightenment ideas. But, we need to ask rather cautiously, what exactly has this made of our world? And what has it made of us? Who are we? When we look at one another what now prompts us to say 'Me Too'?

We could start by looking at two men whose lives spanned the rise of the new thinking: William Pitt the Elder (1708–1778) and William Pitt the Younger (1759–1806) – the latter was educated at home by the former who was his father. The Elder was the prime minister at the time and the son was quite soon going to be the prime minister himself at the astonishing age of 24. Today this surprising concatenation, of a father and son getting on so well with each other (as they did) and of both of them reaching such high office, seems somewhat incredible. It feels like an example of a hangover from an older world. Even in the midst of the Enlightenment, when it was perhaps less extraordinary and may still have been seen as quite a natural thing, it stands out. So we can ask, do the Pitts belong to the World We Have Lost or are they Enlightenment figures?

We know that the father and son were of the same mould, of the same stamp, similar in ways unimaginable to us with our post-Freudian notions of family conflict; they were able to tread the same paths without major dispute; they were of the same class, they had the same education, the same religion, the same views, the same clothes; they were of the same race, height and colour. Looking at each other they must have seen themselves. And that sort of harmony then seemed encouraging to people who wanted to avoid conflict.

But, you will say, this Idyll of the Age of Reason is improbable (did they *never* have a proper disagreement?)

and rare (did *everyone* live such harmonious lives?) and of course highly contingent on their wealth and position. We moderns, struggling in the arguments and contentious trivia of inter-generational conflict in the 2020s ('No Dad, she's an *actor*, we don't say *actress* any more. Why don't you catch up?') can only look back in wonder. But even those who at the time were struggling with smallpox, gin, poverty and puerperal fever at the bottom of the social heap in the slums of Georgian London would have wondered at the phenomenon of the Pitts much less than we do because, although they themselves were living no sort of idyll, they could hardly have imagined the world ever being *very* different from the world they knew.

It has been estimated that in the time of the Pitts less than 1% of the British population was Catholic, and until 1795 even the Methodists were members of the Church of England. The dissensions of the Civil War were far behind, the Revolution Settlement of 1688 was holding and that will-o'-the-wisp the Jacobite Cause had been brushed aside fairly easily in spite of the panics it provoked in 1715 and 1745. *All was well*, perhaps, and certainly all was generally *the same*. Pope summed up an optimistic view, widely-held at the time he wrote, in the most triumphant section of his *Essay on Man*, that 'Whatever is, is right!' It took a Voltaire to see beyond that in his classic (and hilarious) attack on optimism, *Candide* of 1759, the year of Pitt the Younger's birth.

But the new world was coming. The Pitts presided over governments that had to contend with the American Revolution and in the case of William the Younger the French Revolution and Napoleon. The great Age of Reform that would alter everything in the period 1830 to 1890 (everything public that is, from the prisons to the army, from the army to Parliament, from Parliament to the universities, from the universities to the Church, from the Church to a somewhat ramshackle local government which turned into modern councils, and so on) was already showing its teeth in some of the legislation inspired by Pitt and friends of his such as William Wilberforce.

Nonetheless, below the unequal social surface and these political crises a kind of mental harmony still prevailed, *faute de mieux* one might say. Reason, of a sort at least, reduced to *reasonableness* by the conservative temper of the age, was the deep watchword of the day but the incessant reworkings of reason that characterise the modern world were only just beginning. Witchcraft trials were a thing of the past as were executions for blasphemy. Anti-government or anti-monarchical satire could earn you the pillory (not so bad if the mob was on your side) but the days of 'crop-eared Prynne' whose sedition won him the loss of no fewer than two parts of his ears were long past. The monarch was now increasingly constitutional in any case. Voltaire had won his other battle; the *infâme* had been, if not *écrasée*, then at least reduced so that it was less able to perpetrate infamy, and the calm order of the Augustan mind was only becoming calmer as a little sensibility was added to the violent satire of the early part of the century when Swift and Pope had unleashed their *saeva indignatio*. We were on our way to the world of Jane Austen whose novels, for all her insight and in spite of when they were written, never mention the French or American revolutions and barely touch on the Napoleonic War; a good example of the period's capacity for harmonious thinking, in Britain at least. Not many writers who were alive when the news came home from

Passchendaele and the Somme a hundred years later could so blithely have ignored what we think of as 'the history' of their time.

So far, you may say, so good. These were people – I mean the Pitts and their kind – who could truly look at one another and still say Me Too. If there was trouble at election time, and there *were* riots and what we call hate-speech, all parties knew what the score was and it was the same score; there was only one hymn-sheet to sing off after all. The antagonism between George III and Pitt the Younger on the one hand and the future George IV and Charles James Fox on the other looks to us who have lived through the twentieth century like a very local affair – a few well-educated and only moderately corrupt landowners carving up Parliament between them and fixing everything so that the unimaginable *hoi polloi* wouldn't come and spoil the party. But of course my point is that in the eighteenth century the *hoi-polloi* could hardly imagine that things were not *fixed* or that the party wouldn't go on forever.

In the intellectual arena, although the great Hume was denied the chair of philosophy at Edinburgh University, the *casus belli* in his case was not, as people nowadays imagine, that he was an 'atheist' but that he was quite the opposite, being like Pope a deist. There were no atheists to speak of. Newton had explained the universe and had allowed into his picture its Great Original, God, who was necessary as the keystone of the cosmic arch which, for better or worse, was simply what it appeared to be, up there sustaining a whole which wouldn't change and which was, when all was said and done, the only possible and therefore the *right* sort of world.

Most people then thought of a 'station in life' as an inevitable, and not always altogether a bad thing. Most people agreed that more empire would be better empire, better for Britain and equally better for the native inhabitants of the countries ruled. Everyone thought that people would remain unequal even in the most equal of circumstances, as witness the thoroughgoing Enlightenment Englishmen who, having brought about the American Revolution, declared natural liberty for all but continued to keep slaves.

There is no call to paint eighteenth-century Europe as some kind of lost Earthly Paradise, far from it, but it *is* necessary to portray it as the last period of British history (at least) in which a certain ineluctable unanimity was the prevalent mode of thought, a time when most people were, more or less, able to see 'Me' in each other. As in the Pitt-vs-Fox and Hume-vs-the Kirk conflicts mentioned above, this unanimity was evident even when Enlightenment figures were in conflict with each other: from the perspective of today the thing most like an eighteenth-century Whig in the whole world is an eighteenth-century Tory. Compared with the differences between Buddhists, agnostics, Muslims, atheists, born-again Christians, New Agers, Catholics and people who give their religion as 'Jedi' in today's Britain, the intellectual distinction between one eighteenth-century British Christian and another (Anglican, Catholic or Presbyterian) was quite negligible whatever the parties concerned thought of it at the time, and the atheists only existed in the imaginations of polemicists against religious positions they disagreed with. The Whig and Tory groups in the Commons were described as being like two carriages driving side by side along the same road. However it seemed to the participants in these miniature wars, the reality was that there was a deep harmony, an essential ontological view of the world that could not greatly vary. Perhaps in 1750 and even for the rest of the eighteenth century ninety per cent of the British population would have been able, surface differences aside, to look round at each other and more or less universally say 'Me Too'.

A classic example of this unanimity was demonstrated during the war against Napoleon when the House of Commons sat, as it often then did, all night. Towards the end of a long debate (great orators such as Burke and Sheridan could easily speak for two hours at a stretch) the Member on his feet, banging away at some then-important issue, stopped, looked up at a window and saw that the sun was rising. Without a pause he broke into Latin and quoted a famous passage about dawn which, it appears, most members of the House recognised and approved. Unanimity was in that deep sense complete, the debate came to an end and such wounds as had been inflicted were forgotten in a moment of mutual satisfaction among people who had, of course, all had exactly the same education at a number of remarkably similar schools and at the same two universities. Looking at one another, these white, adult, land-owning, upper-middle-class and upper-class males, all gentlemen and all dressed much alike, would have felt 'I got that quotation! I'm like him. He's like me.' Nobody would have thought of laughing at such snobbery or exclusiveness as may have been involved; even those who didn't recognise the quotation would have *wanted* to be able to say 'Me Too'.

It is an interesting question to ask how many citizens going about their business outside the House of Commons in London that day would have found this story offensive, or rather how few. It is hard to imagine, even in the age of

The Dunciad, someone with a ukulele greeting Pitt with a song of which the refrain was 'Fuck off back to Eton', as happened to David Cameron more than once, and that would not just be because Pitt wasn't an Etonian. Not many voices were raised against the general hierarchical situation then in operation and support for an entirely different form of education or politics was minimal. In his day the French and American revolutions had come and gone; their effect would be tremendous, but not until a century later. In some deep sense 'Enlightenment Man', however unenlightened any *individual* man or woman might have been, recognised himself or herself wherever they looked.

The Enlightenment came out of this world of deep intellectual stability and it is marked by its essentialist ideas of Moral Sense (I think of Shaftesbury's *Inquiry into Virtue* of 1712) and the obviousness of the best social arrangements. Much will now change and the nineteenth century will reform everything, but even those changes will for a long time remain within the parameters adumbrated by the Age of Reason and its method.

And where are we now? Since 1800 we have of course been through Romanticism, the Industrial Revolution, Darwin, the Victorian Loss of Faith, the expansion and loss of the world's biggest-ever empire, the First and Second World Wars, the radical shrinking of the globe (my grandfather took at least three weeks to get to India where he passed his whole career; now we get to New Zealand in a day) and the invention of the telephone, the radio, the motor car, television, the aeroplane, the microchip, the mobile phone, the computer, the internet *et tout le bazar*. We live on Facebook and Instagram; we expect to see the same shops in Manila, Durban, Recife, Seoul, Anchorage,

Vladivostok and Delhi, and we expect our mobile phones to work in all those locations, connecting us more or less instantly with our banks and with our 'loved ones' and 'partners' (significant new terms) everywhere on the globe.

In modern times when we come across an example of the old harmony and community, in for instance the world of the coal-miners in Britain up to the 1980s, we can see clearly how one cannot go backwards and forwards at the same time. A great deal of heat is engendered by the notion that Mrs Thatcher 'smashed' the British coal industry in 1984, but by then their days were numbered whichever prime minister was in power – Harold Wilson had in fact closed more pits than Thatcher would. Like the House of Commons under Pitt, the miners were 'close-knit' (to use the cliché here) and formed, indeed, a community. But it is one that, as the years go by and hindsight becomes clearer, looks as antiquated as the communities of the Middle Ages. Miners certainly looked at one another and said 'Me Too' in almost all aspects of their lives, but technological developments and social changes would have brought about the destruction of their community under almost any circumstances. Above all the *intellectual underpinnings* of the old order where 'communities' existed had vanished. History moves on, and it is currently moving towards fewer and fewer obvious, anchored, time-tested identities. The children of those miners are none of them miners themselves, nor do they live in any recognisable 'community'. Most of them, surely, now work in IT or marketing or the NHS and live in Milton Keynes or Oldham or East Kilbride.

How on earth have we come so far so fast? And has it been danger-free to travel at that speed? These are otiose questions; we have done what we have done at the speed that it took – there are no automatic *limitations de vitesse* in culture; there is no reason to find one speed more natural than another. If we feel that things have rushed upon us recently it may only be because change was slower and thus rather less noticeable in 'the old days'. And as we look back at the last generation of intellectually harmonious people, the inhabitants of the Enlightenment who, if they quarrelled on the surface, profoundly *thought alike*, the question becomes: if we are not like them, what are we? I mean, do we want a unanimity to put in the place of that of our ancestors? Or have we changed into chameleons and thus changed like chameleons as all around us has changed? *Tempora mutantur et nos mutamur in illis*? Who now is the same as me? With whom can I sincerely identify? Is *anybody* now Me Too? Is everybody?

As usual there are optimists and pessimists offering answers to these questions. People for whom the *restrictions* involved in the old senses of identity have been removed must feel optimistic; the new freedom of choice, speech and thought has brought with it a freedom of identity for women, who in nearly all previous generations would have been without much career choice, and for sons of immigrant Hindu bus drivers who feel free to put themselves forward for election to Parliament without apology and become chancellor of the exchequer without anyone turning a hair, lesbians who want to marry and have babies – these present arrangements, far out of line with so much previous thinking though they are, do definitely suit many people. And the old thinking, the world we have so definitely and completely left behind, seems hardly to matter to such. 'Millennial' women who came of age around the year 2000 are faintly aware that as recently as 1950 they would have had to put their boyfriends up to their parents for approval before going out with them or thinking of marrying them, and everyone then assumed that they *would* marry if they wanted to co-habit. But they don't lose any sleep over this knowledge, they aren't disturbed by it, it plays no part in their self-assessment or their decision-making, it's just as if things had never been different from how they are today. They take a pitying backward glance at their grandparents' generation and then they're off, away without a second look. Some of the parents one meets today express gratitude that their offspring have even bothered to *mention* to them that they were getting married.

The pessimists, on the other hand, see urbanisation and globalisation, along with the new individual freedoms of the many, as a loss of order, a loss of identity, perhaps a loss of dignity and certainly of deference. They lament the passing of a quieter and simpler world where they could recognise and understand their neighbours, their institutions, their leaders and their country. They have also begun to feel that they are on 'the wrong side of history' in Barack Obama's phrase, and see huge forces arrayed against them.

I am very far from judging. It is too early to tell whether the new arrangements are 'better' or 'worse' than the old – and how would we know? But the important thing in the human quest for self-knowledge is to find out who we think we are; and an inevitable step in that process is to ask which other people *we are like.* Thus we now need to ask such questions as Who are they, these women and their 'partners'? Who are they like? Who are *we* now? What is our *point de repère*? Of whom can we say that *that is me too*? We used to know, more or less unthinkingly in many cases, who we were, but now it's much harder. Hegel was right, history cannot go backwards and there is no retreat in time; the new consensus cannot be reversed. But wherever it takes us people will always manage to find someone or something to identify with. We can only ask where it will come from.

4. 'Je Suis Charlie'

Enlightenment looks a little different from the perspective of France, not socially but intellectually. There are assumptions made in French culture that may help us answer some of our questions and perhaps we need to refresh our knowledge of modern French thinking, say the thinking of the seventy years between the Second World War and today, thus perhaps from Jean-Paul Sartre's first major publication, *L'Etre et le Néant* of 1942 to the death of Jacques Derrida in 2003, and beyond to the coronavirus of 2020.

Sartre has lost credibility because of many things, among them his treatment of Simone de Beauvoir, but as with most philosophers there are good ideas to be found in his work even if one has to plough through a great deal of less interesting material before unearthing them. These include an attack on the very idea of identity, and not just the identities of people but the identities of everything whatever. 'There is no love' declared the guru of the Left Bank, 'apart from the deeds of love.' True enough – love isn't a thing that one can define *a priori* and more or less approximate to by way of asking such questions as 'Is this really love?', 'Is this better love than last time?' or 'Have I captured the essence of love?' 'Love' can only be all the actions, thoughts and words that have gone to make up our idea of love since the concept arrived in Western culture in southern France in the tenth century. As J-PS himself famously said, 'existence precedes essence', so we won't know what the essence or definition of love 'really' was until the last lover dies and then it will just be an amalgam of all the ideas of love collected over the millennia. It exists, but its essence is pretty much non-existent. We'll only know what it was when there is nobody left to know what it was.

There are no essences. So 'France', for instance, is obviously *made-up*, a construct, not some essential place that one can find by visiting or, more often, miss during a visit; and the same applies to Justice or History or Society or Evil or Education. None of these things has any existence outside the ever-changing human definitions of them and example can always be added to example (*'That* isn't really evil!' 'There's *no such thing* as society!' Or, as John Gray has written, 'There's no such thing as humanity') in an always-unstable process. And this means that for each of us humans there can't be any essential Identity either. It seems clear that modern thought is ever more Nominalist: 'France' and 'Justice', like 'Love', are not Platonic Forms or Ideas, they are merely *names we've chosen*. But then what of us? Who, after all, am 'I' going to be? Who are *you*? Really? '*Finally*'?

Ideas such as these set about destroying many of the fundamentals of Western philosophy in the second half of the twentieth century. Buckets of ink had been spilled, from Plato to A. J. Ayer, on topics such as 'What is a person?' or 'What is the Good?' or 'What is *sense*?' But these must now be seen as pointless enquiries. When we moved from Sartre, Existentialism and Structuralism to Poststructuralism and Derrida the ground beneath our feet, already shaky, gave way completely. There are now no 'positive' terms in language, no Truth to be spoken. All essentialist thinking is metaphysical eyewash, relating to nothing real. Language is all, and language is, in the end, nothing either, or at least *not an essential thing*. It can at any rate not successfully describe any essence.

If we are to take our enquiry into *who we are* seriously in the light of these modern philosophies, much derided though they may have been at Oxford and other bastions of the Anglo-American analytical tradition (in 1992 Cambridge came within a whisker of refusing Derrida an honorary doctorate), we are going to have to accept that we are nothing essential and that concepts such as the Soul or the Self or Identity are simply metaphors, or even unnecessary additions to our thinking. As a result it follows that we may be *radically unable* to say 'Me Too' in any kind of ontological or essential recognition of an Other that is in some way *also truly me*. For if even 'I' am not *truly* me, where then does that leave *us*?

On the positive side, we are left with freedom, or 'condemned to freedom' as Sartre put it, the freedom to choose whatever we like, and this brings both advantages and disadvantages. One advantage is the obvious one that we are no longer forced to 'be' something that we prefer not to be, as so many people were in centuries gone by, and this must be an improvement. To be an enclosed nun, perhaps against one's will and perhaps without being a real believer, or to be forced to pretend to toe the party line under Stalin, or mouth unpalatable words at the point of a gun under Mao or Pol Pot or the Kims of North Korea, or to be obliged to marry a person one detests or pretend to be attracted to the opposite sex when one isn't, these seem to us to be the opposite of any sort of human life that is worth living. *Viva la libertà*! On the other hand, as Nietzsche put it, the question for us is not so much what we are now free *from* (religious dogmas, social pressures, totalitarian regimes, absolute parental authority and so on, that's obvious) but what we are free *for*.

If there is no single definite thing that I am then I do not have a stable identity. If I am not *essentially* anything then the claim that I *am* English or a Man or Catholic or an Intellectual or a Banker or Good or White has lost its compelling force. I could stop being any one of these things, however painful it might be, at any time. Glossing Sartre on this topic I suggest that his famous example of the café waiter (one imagines he had Paris in mind) reveals more than he intended. He claims that a waiter must *play the part* of a waiter and points out that nobody could 'authentically' be a waiter. So far so good, but then whenever the waiter is at home 'being a husband' or 'being a father' he must also play the part required and fulfil (or is it just *imitate*?) the role of spouse or parent. But when then can he ever become 'authentic'? The answer is *never*. He is able to break free, to give up waiting perhaps, but he is then obliged in some measure to play a new part, say that of an unemployed ex-waiter, or the part of a member of his new profession whatever that is. He can't just 'be himself' for there is no such thing. He can be free *from* but never truly free *for* anything; whatever he falls into will be another trap or illusion or inauthentic role.

To come more up-to-date we could consider the slogan '*Je suis Charlie*' which appeared in the aftermath of one of several terrorist atrocities committed by Muslim extremists in Paris in the 2010s. It seems that the killers, who sprayed the offices of the satirical magazine *Charlie Hebdo* with sufficient machine-gun fire to kill thirteen members of staff, themselves had no identity problem at all. They knew exactly who they were, where they were going, what they were doing. And this provides a template for others who identify with them. It is a choice of course, and one can very well choose to be a law-abiding anti-terrorist Muslim. But clearly some Muslims, especially young Muslim men, do identify to some degree with the *Jihad* being waged by ISIS, Al-Qaeda, Boko Haram, and the many other terror groups. The hundreds of thousands of people who have turned out repeatedly on the streets of Karachi and Islamabad in the last decade to protest against the 'blasphemy' committed by Asia Bibi (a Christian Pakistani lady who made a disparaging comment about Mohammed to her neighbours) and thrust a sea of banners into the air bearing the words '*Hang Asia Bibi*' in English and Urdu were surely not entirely unhappy to see the Twin Towers come down and the blasphemous journalists of *Charlie Hebdo* duly punished. '*Me too*' they must have thought or, if not, where does the wide international recruitment for the Muslim terrorist groups come from? Here is identity, the old-fashioned kind, with a quite literal vengeance.

It looks very much as if the liberal optimism that declares that 'Muslims are not terrorists' is insufficiently aware of who identifies with whom in the modern world. The young Pakistani men who screamed for Asia Bibi's blood, effectively keeping her unsentenced and in solitary confinement for eight years, and cheered when they heard that a politician opposed to the blasphemy laws had been murdered, were surely saying that the terror campaign being waged around the world in the name of Islam was their struggle too. '*Me too*' is effectively what '*Hang Asia Bibi*' is proclaiming.

On the other side of the fence huge numbers of Europeans put up badges at the time of the Paris massacre proclaiming '*Je suis Charlie*' – almost precisely the same gesture made by the actual Me Too movement in France. One French slogan for that movement to protect women was '*Touche pas à mon pote*' which translates as 'Hands off my pal.' My pal. *My* pal. Mine. *Me*. She's who I am. She's me.

But some French people, when '*Je*' was being '*Charlie*' all over the globe, took the trouble to say to me '*Mais moi – je ne suis pas Charlie!*' They were not, surely, indicating support for the Muslim gunmen; instead they were showing a political preference for a calmer and less offensive tone of debate than that employed by a rather scurrilous and humourless satirical magazine. Their self-proclaimed identity as *not* Charlie was a choice, but of what? Of, presumably, another France, one with less tolerance of the violently-expressed criticism found in the pages of *Charlie Hebdo*. They did not want it to be assumed that, just because violence had been inflicted on the staff of the magazine, we all had to support its methods and opinions. They set up a small intellectual camp on the conservative side, drawing a line in the sand: 'We don't like terrorism, but we're not on the side of the anything-goes culture of the modern satirical magazine.'

The existentialists taught us that we always have a choice – indeed that we are radically obliged to make a choice because not choosing is also a choice, a choice for the status quo. This lesson has now been deeply learned. The 'doing your own thing' and the 'expressing yourself' of the 1960s have flowered into the loud public proclamation of rights, the claims of identity and the denunciations of injustice that we have come to see all around us. What is paradoxical, and this is the crux of my argument here, is that now the only way to declare that you are 'yourself' and that you have a right to 'be yourself' is to *identify with others*. We once unthinkingly belonged in our places and societies, and then the Enlightenment slowly showed us that our belonging was not natural or God-given and certainly not inevitable. We are now free of such belongings and can make ourselves up; we have set about trying to do just that and the way we do it is by demanding recognition for 'our' group and demonstrating our attachment to it and crying that it is us. We are members, self-proclaimed members, of 'the gay community' or 'the Jewish community' or 'the Indigenous American community', 'the Uber-drivers community', 'the football community' and so on. The risk is that this will bring about ever-increasing social fragmentation – as in the great divide in the USA between Democrats and Republicans of which the least effect is that one cannot invite people from different sides of the political divide to dinner at the same time.

So, confronted with a 'campaign' to signal opposition to an event (in the case of the *Charlie Hebdo* atrocity quite reasonable opposition) we feel obliged to put up our own badges and see ourselves as a 'campaign' too. We think we are becoming ourselves first by imitating our opponents and then by doing exactly the same things as the other people on 'our side' are doing. Hence the taste for demonstrations and the high probability that each demonstration will bring out the 'militants' from the opposing camp.

Soft liberal optimists such as myself might now recognise that, as we don't have to belong to anything or anyone any more (I think of the children who in recent years have tried to divorce their parents) we can all belong to each other. 'Ah, there's a human!' we can now say, and, after a pause, 'I'm one too.' This would have pleased Enlightenment thinkers a great deal, but if it *seems* closer to realisation in the modern world it may in reality be much further away. On the one hand no serious thinkers today are likely to suggest that other kinds of human who do not resemble them in some way are for that reason 'less human' or significantly different; on the other hand when we decide that a difference has been unfairly created or emphasised we become very angry and, in this Age of Indignation, climb onto our hobbyhorses and go into immoderate battle defending our real or perceived differences.

Hence the exaggeration and polarisation of political life. Recognising that the other is sometimes and somehow 'me' is an aid to harmony and tolerance, but now that instead of the old identifications I am offered such clubs as those that have spuriously formed around my race or my sexual orientation (empty vessels in the end) I may prefer the freedom of going without. The freedom to 'be me' is an aim or goal forever incomplete; but now that we are able to question everything let's not decide too quickly on what the right answers are. The sacred cows of the new left consensus may not be carrying every jot and tittle of The Truth after all. Not for me. Not even if I am quite alone.

5. The Importance of History

In the face of the convulsions currently besetting the West and much of the planet, and in spite of all, perhaps a renewed humanism is possible, an improved 'woke' approach that lets me identify with all of my species? *Nihil humani a me alienum puto* and all that? Let us see.

When we talk of humans and tell the story of us *homines*, or at least of us *Homo sapiens* in our most recent phase, we are talking history; and as we have seen history is one of the least-ostentatious but most far-reaching products of the Enlightenment. The Age of Reason spent time inventing how to do history and we have done it in the same way ever since, history being, as we should expect, the *science* of the written past that includes the study of evidence, the faithful reconstruction of what has happened to us during the last five thousand years supplemented by the anthropology and archaeology which take the story back a lot further. History, archaeology and anthropology are mainstream university disciplines, and they are all children of eighteenth-century thinking.

But, like science itself, history is never neutral as we now know. So there is a meta-level at which we feel the need to consider *historiography*, the rational discussion of how history can best be written and what counts as historical knowledge. Thus we hope to increase our chances of saying something more accurate and more useful about ourselves in the past tense. We ask whether we should be considering 'kings and battles' as our central area of research or whether statistics concerning trade might not be more important; we consider the detailed lives of medieval peasants, as revealed in the records of the Inquisition, to build up painstaking pictures of their lives at the humblest level.[3] And recently huge efforts have been made, sometimes sensibly and sometimes tendentiously, to establish that the histories of women or of non-white people have been suppressed or ignored.

But political correctness has introduced a new danger: we have become obsessed by this meta-level (historiography – the level of 'how?') and ignored the *history* (the level of 'what?') on the grounds that you can't choose what to say before you have decided what is most important, 'correct' and useful to say. We are so anxious to *say the right things* (right from the point of view of present-day thinking) that we fail to apply common sense to past events, ideas and changes. The obvious example is 'Eurocentrism' which was the writing of non-European history as though it were merely a footnote to the 'real' history taking place in Europe; this is now seen as a terrible intellectual vice. What's wrong with it apparently is that it looks at everything from the perspective of the West, of the White Man, of European dominance, and it must therefore be corrected. What is bad about Eurocentric history, according to its critics, is that it is written by and for the wrong people. But reorganising history backwards in

---

3 See Emmanuel Le Roy Ladurie, *Montaillou*, 1975 (English translation 1978) for an example.

this way, looking for 'other voices' in the past, though it has some obvious advantages, has its pitfalls.

A good example was provided by the British prime minister Tony Blair when he famously or notoriously chose to make a proclamation 'apologising for slavery'. His rather hasty glance at the history of the slave trade, in which Britain played a large part in the seventeenth and eighteenth centuries, had him reaching for his conscience and a microphone, keen to make amends for the horrors inflicted on Africans by his countrymen two hundred years earlier.

Modern thinking has concluded that slavery was an unmitigated evil and there is no need to argue with that. But historiographical considerations, roughly meaning 'what *kind of thing* we should write about' and 'how we should approach the past event or process under consideration', clearly distorted Blair's thinking in his *bien-pensant* but faintly ludicrous performance. Slavery is too suspiciously topical for us to have expected him to be objective and his approach was undoubtedly one-sided, but we should be more worried that it was a topic that he felt 'needed to be addressed' *at all*. The sheer *badness* of the trade overwhelmed his judgement I suppose, leading him to focus on that badness exclusively while failing to appreciate its total history. For *everything* 'needs to be addressed' if you can find out enough about it – the past being an endless and endlessly-revised story. 'Total history' is only a mythical ambition and it will never be written although it is an honourable project which, like the ambition of science, will never explain everything but whose aim remains to consider the *whole* of the natural universe; warts, puzzles and all. An attempt in that direction would, in any event, be a lot better than partial history of the Blair kind.

A history teacher said to me recently that he thought that slavery should be taught in British schools instead of the usual diet of 'the Tudors and the First World War'. Clearly this historiographical suggestion was made with a definite moral purpose in mind; my friend the history teacher wanted British children to learn about the shame of their ancestors instead of about less uncomfortable topics. But why?

There can be no objection to research and teaching being directed to any historical topic, including of course slavery. But in reality time constrains the curriculum and choices have to be made. Now if one were arbitrarily to divide British history into one hundred parts and choose a few decades or topics from among them for school education one might prefer to teach any number of things rather than slavery. Since less than three per cent of the UK population can possibly be descended from slaves and these descendants have only been in Britain in any numbers since 1950 it is not obvious that teaching about slavery is a historical topic particularly relevant to the children's lives. It should not be ignored, but if it is covered it should obviously (in a 'British History' course) be in the general context of the 'history of our country' of which it constitutes, at a generous estimate, about a quarter of one per cent of those one hundred units as calculated on any normal basis.

But relevance or even historical coverage are presumably not really the criteria here; what is at stake is morality. Teaching man's inhumanity to man, especially when the inhumanity has been perpetrated by fellow-citizens, seems to me to be a very good idea. But teaching one example of this *as history* is wildly distorting and gives it undue historical importance even if it has great moral importance. It is a selection of a topic that is cruder than, say, a history of the monasteries in the Middle Ages or a history of the Industrial Revolution, because it selects one part of a total mentality and isolates it for people to tut and agonise over. The equivalent would be to teach the history of Genghis Khan's cruelties without considering the intellectual condition of twelfth-century Mongolia, Genghis's relations with China, his religion, normal military tactics at the time, questions of trade and a wide variety of other things. You will say 'Well all that other stuff could be built around the course on slavery' to which I reply, 'Yes, it could.' But (a) do you think it *would* be so built in a fifth-form 'slavery' class? Would there be time? and (b), more importantly, would any sane history teacher set about making cruelty in a given period of Mongolian history the focus of his or her teaching? Would that not be Retrospective Interference revealing a *parti pris*?

The fact is that 'teaching slavery' is likely to be taken as an opportunity to use an interesting historical subject for political propaganda purposes. It is instructive in this connection to consider the propaganda produced in large quantity by the British media during the Napoleonic War. The 'Corsican tyrant' was lampooned, called the worst possible names and considered the devil incarnate. Now that the threat of French invasion, complete with stories of rape and plunder, has diminished (since 1804) our attitude towards him has cooled down and we can be objective, enlightened and historically scientific about him and his adventure. Stirring up animus has no place in a serious history class and we wouldn't dream of doing it about

Napoleon any more. Its place would be in a *philosophy* class concerned with morality, nationality, responsibility, identity and the like.

I have twice met millennial German ladies who shocked me in the same way. Both were deeply disenchanted by their school education (the best in Europe in other respects of course) to the point that they had left Germany and were now permanently living in France and Scotland respectively. In both cases they felt that the obsession with the Third Reich, endlessly repeated as 'history' year after year in their classrooms, had made them feel ashamed of being German, mentally distressed, self-hating, horrified by their own families, paranoid about the outer world and, to cap it all, almost entirely ignorant about any other history than that of Hitler. Their view of their country's past had been captured by a twelve-year period (1933–45). Their view of human history and of themselves was coloured a horrible grey that shaded into bloody black.

Nobody believes that history is simply the story of 'man's inhumanity to man', and surely nobody believes that the 'mentalities', as the French call them, of people and cultures are constant. With every age in every country come a number of presuppositions by which the denizens of the time and place must be judged, if we are to judge them at all – and most of the time the judgement must be Not Proven, to quote that anomalous but useful Scottish verdict.

The people who organised and profited from the slave trade were different from us and, one must suppose, as moral according to their own lights as we are according to ours. They were not booed in church or spat at in the streets for being monsters; they had monuments erected to them and when they offered financial help to charities and universities it was gratefully received; no conscience-stricken movements arose to condemn them *toto caelo*. Not then. And once the *Zeitgeist* had changed against them they were quick to change their habits and support the British Navy as it set about extirpating slave traders from the Atlantic. Having taken the lead one way they took the lead in the other. Their consciences were clearly flexible. Any other view involves Retrospective Interference.[4]

We remain today in the grip of the Whig interpretation of history. The successes of the Enlightenment, the Industrial Revolution and twentieth-century science have confirmed us in our dubious belief that things get better and better, that there is an inevitable element of amelioration in the march of history. We were very struck by Barack Obama's campaign slogan, at least when he won his first election: 'Yes we can!' he cried to his adoring supporters who gave it back to him at full volume and then, as if to answer the question 'We can *what*?', he supplied his often-repeated answer: '*Change!*' Other politicians have taken up this word since and *Change* has become a modern mantra, equivalent to the Victorian notion of Progress as trumpeted by the historian Macaulay and his like. All change is now good, all economic and social thought is dominated by the notion of 'growth', every corner of every country needs 'development'.

But these notions were entirely unknown to the Age of Reason. The assumption made by such thinkers and writers as Pope, Voltaire, Swift and Hume was that there was rubbish to be cleared away – abuses, injustices, inequalities,

---

[4] 'Education is not indoctrination. Our history is not a blank page on which we can write our own version of what it should have been according to our contemporary views and prejudice.' (Rip MacKenzie)

terrible poverty – but the answer to them was not a change *forward* but instead the re-establishment of something more natural or classically-approved, a change *back* to a golden age of simplicity. It comes as quite a shock when, in the third book of *Gulliver's Travels*, a magician shows Gulliver a moving image of the Roman Senate; our hero is impressed by the great and noble politicians of Antiquity, but when he asks to see a modern parliament in action he is disgusted by the venality, corruption, place-seeking and stupidity of the MPs. The plea is for us to go back to Roman republican virtue, or to some sort of Early Christian simplicity. And similarly with Rousseau, whose programme is even more radical when he suggests that we should look back to the Noble Savage and discard all this horrible modernity. Even Voltaire wants to *écraser l'infâme* without much mention of the improvements that would replace it; and he preferred England to France because the English were sensible and modest in an old-fashioned sort of way, not because they represented some Utopian future.[5]

Given this static view of history the thought that Change (or *Reform*, the great Victorian watchword) was automatically a good thing was very far from the Enlightenment mind. The desirability of change is something we have learnt since, and we should recognise that the views of our ancestors were very different from our own. The people who wanted Blair to apologise for slavery were as deeply imbued with their own opinions as Enlightenment man was – and if for our part we think that

---

5 See his *Lettres sur les anglais* of 1733. Another shock is available chez Karl Marx who waxes lyrical in several places about the unalienated and harmonious life of the Middle Ages. His target was nineteenth-century industrialisation, not '*the past*'.

Enlightenment man had an insufficient desire for change he would most certainly have thought that our obsession with it was unhealthy.[6]

That Enlightenment man was largely '*man*' shows another profound difference between him and us. It was almost completely unimaginable in the eighteenth century to conceive that women could be the same as men in most respects or were entirely equal in others; according to Lord Chesterfield they were 'children of a larger growth'. Similarly it was unimaginable then to see animals as 'species' that might need to be 'protected', or to see that homosexuals might have 'rights'. We are so completely convinced of our own rightness in these matters that it is now impossible for us to see past our own views, but intelligent men of good will once held opinions opposite to ours with as much honesty as we can muster ourselves.

So: must change always axiomatically and automatically be good? Surely history teaches us otherwise. Those apologising for slavery are quite right to consider the slaves first and foremost, the men and women who clearly suffered abominably, but the immediate condemnation of the slave-*shippers* is slightly less obviously right and the removal of their names and statues from buildings is the removal of history itself. Apologies by those who have never been in the relevant situation in the past and have never felt as our ancestors felt is a pointless exercise and a denial of reality. The names and statues that the 'woke' wish to erase do

---

6 An example here is medicine. We now think that bigger, better equipment and snazzier treatments are obviously the answer to medical problems, and we look to the future for a cure for cancer for instance. Eighteenth-century literature, and especially its poetry, is full of pastoral texts suggesting that going back to the country and leading a purer and simpler life will cure most ills.

not commemorate slavery or the slavers' involvement in it – they commemorate benevolence. It may be a kind of benevolence that we regard as a great deal less significant than the slavery which provided the money with which it was put into practice, but have we forgotten the principle on which all modern morality rests? Kant's thesis? He, if you remember, proposes that we should judge the morality of an action not by its intrinsic merits but according to the intentions of the actor.

When, outside Kings' College Cambridge, we look at the rather good but also rather surprising statue of Henry VIII we are inclined to wonder: Why *him*? Henry was guilty of murder, torture and other brutalities as well as the destruction of the monasteries on which much that was best in the life of humbler English country-folk depended; he trumped up charges against the innocent and had them put to death in horrible ways, laid waste to northern England in the wake of the Pilgrimage of Grace and did all that he did in the service of his own great ego.[7] A monster in short.

One notices no objections to the statue of this king who was the college's second founder (the first was the rather nicer Henry VI who came, as every schoolboy knows, in three parts) because it is regarded, by those who know anything about it, as *historical*, and thus as *hors de combat*. But this is only because we no longer care about Catholic–Protestant conflicts or the politics of the Renaissance while caring, at once deeply and in a rather shallow way, about

---

7 Henry holds the record for the Bloodiest Tudor. Even-handedly executing those he considered too Catholic and too Presbyterian, as well as killing numerous other opponents and wives (along with some of their lovers), his tally outstrips that of his daughters by far, reaching 57,000 executions during his reign, a number revised by some historians who propose the figure of 72,000.

the plight of people of a different race and their treatment. We are obsessed by race as previous centuries were by religion and we are thus blinded to the parallel between these two obsessions.

Religious disharmony resulted in Europe's most murderous war (allowing for the population difference), the Thirty Years War of 1618–48. We think we are now above that, but it is a failure in our liberal consciences that we do not condemn the religious causes of serious modern disharmony, the so-called spiritual things that lead to violence. The causes of violence indeed include historical racial tensions, but also and perhaps more importantly the aggressive behaviour of non-democratic countries such as Russia and China and the neo-colonial exploitation of the developing world by China and the USA; but they are also to be found in Muslim fundamentalism, in our acceptance of the grotesque situation in the Middle East, in the behaviour of the many dreadful governments of Africa and Asia, and in the tidal wave of migration to Europe. All these things have a history that is not simple and is not to be rectified by wishful thinking in the present.

6. Proust's Way

What must we now *add* to modern thought (that is, developed Enlightenment thought) to make some headway against the current tsunami of hatred and divisive politically-correct thinking? It looks as if it should be something that will respect an older wisdom but which will avoid throwing away the best advantages of where we are now. We could start by diminishing our assault on the planet, and we should obviously try to limit the population of the world and the over-population of Europe in particular before it is too late, but the communication revolution is here to stay, surely, and we are not going to turn our backs on the knowledge or the medical successes we have now.[8]

In what follows in the second part of this collection of essays I am going to try to indicate some problems with our modern consciousness and suggest some different ways of seeing things. This will be less political than what has gone before because I think our problems are more widespread than that. To take us away from immediate questions, then, I would like to turn to one of the most challenging writers of the modern world, writer of what one critic has called 'the Bible of Humanity'.

---

8 In spite of this concession to current intellectual norms it is worth pointing out that the third most dangerous thing you can do medically (after having heart disease or cancer) is to go into hospital.

Please bear with me as I retreat into a reading of Proust. '*Proust?*' you cry. '*At this time of day? Ye gods.*' But so it is. The further away he is from us the better he is for us, I'd suggest. Let me depress you further with a hint of what I mean: Proust's great novel is much too short. This, one has to admit, is not a popular opinion, but if you ask anyone who has read it what *A la recherche du temps perdu* is about you may find them telling you that it should be a great deal longer. Really. Longer.[9]

Let's say for example that we are following Marcel during his walk along the Vivonne which occurs towards the end of 'Combray', the first section of the novel, the one which focuses on the narrator's childhood. Young Marcel, as we may call him, takes many such walks, trotting with his parents on summer afternoons along what they call the 'Guermantes Way' because the path goes past the Guermantes family *château*. Sometimes he goes by himself, but here he conflates all his walks into a lengthy passage describing the river and the thoughts that it has provoked and still provokes in him. He writes of buttercups, a fisherman whose name he doesn't know, the way the summer rain falls, how nice it would be to have a boat and lie in the bottom and drift with the current, how the bridge reverts to a towpath once you are over the river, how there are 'houses of pleasure' isolated along its banks where overdressed young ladies are to be seen, escapees from shameful affairs in Paris, and how he has sat for hours by the river reading and thinking of his

---

9 In February 1922, the year of his death, Proust wrote to Gallimard saying that he wanted to add more volumes to the already enormous novel. '*A la recherche du temps perdu* is scarcely beginning' he said.

future. I could quote the description *in extenso* but I'll spare you that as I'll need to do it later with another passage.

Any reader can see among these day-dreamings that Proust is not writing about the politics, the economics, the social tensions or the rural problems of the *Belle Epoque*. No Balzac he. There's no Enlightenment Project going on here. But he isn't altogether *not* writing about them either – for they are vaguely present somewhere in the deep background rather than totally absent; not ignored but in their proper place. The passage in question isn't fantasy – very far from it – and I would claim instead that it is a profound sort of realism, but also that it is realism about *something different*. What it is *not* is Enlightenment writing: it isn't explanatory, rational, logical. However, if you will allow this, Proust has always seemed to me to be *writing about enlightenment*. Note the capital E and the lower-case 'e' in these two sentences.

The walk by the Vivonne is very alive (hence the name of the river perhaps). The boy, or perhaps the man remembering the boy, are not figments or detached elements or in some other realm; they are not fantasy; rather they are moments in Marcel's life and *they are me* as I read the pages. And they are you when you read the pages, and potentially all of us.

Would anyone really want to maintain that Marcel's thoughts, the stream of his ideas and feelings as he walks by the stream, are in some unexplained way *lesser* than, say, a study of class distinctions under the Third Republic? Or less important than a book dealing, *à la* Zola, with the economic crises provoked by industrialisation and the Franco-Prussian War? Or less 'real' than a history of painting and design in the Belle Epoque? Can we really say, using the touchstone of personal experience, that the buttercups are less important than the production statistics of the Gobelins factory during Proust's lifetime? Have we made a deep mistake about what is important, what is serious and who we are?

A serious novel extending over 3,000 pages which is not devoted to social realism or the politically correct must of course be about *something*; but what? Morality perhaps? People have felt that there seem to be faint hints of some sort of implicit morality concealed in Proust's pages, hard to find yet surely in there somewhere. And the final volume, when we get to it, will probably demonstrate something about how to live, how to relate to other people, and it might even talk to us about What is Important in Life. No? But we can put off interpretation until then because, with so clever a writer, there must be a kind of moral meaning which we can unearth sooner after all the long digging. There must be – otherwise why write? But can anyone say what it is?

Well, if not Morality then perhaps this is Art for Art's Sake? As Beckett will do about Joyce's *Finnegans Wake*, we could claim that *A la recherche* 'is not *about* something, it *is* that something itself'. With its beautiful descriptions of places and people and with its prose poems on what seem at first to be slight subjects perhaps we are meant to see Proust's text in the same way as we look at a Michelangelo or Monet or even Miró, that is as an art object that exists independently of any interpretation or vulgar meaning.

Or perhaps the abundance of insightful details in Proust's great work can be used to imply something about the intellectual situation in late-nineteenth-century France? This would be a superior version of Realism perhaps. And then of course the whole thing, contemporary with Freud as it is, could be seen as an example of the Psychological Novel.

All of that is perfectly legitimate. After all, there are no police on the planet of Literary Interpretation and no ultimate arbiters. One *could* read Homer to find out about Greek armour, or Milton to find the balance between Greek, Latin and Hebrew learning among the Puritans of the seventeenth century, or Dickens to learn about Victorian furniture. Who is to say one nay in such matters? But still, the huge thrust of the self-writing that is Proust, that vast compendium of digested matter, surely cannot be there only for these smaller purposes. So what *is* it there for?

Well – and I feel like Henry James when he describes his tubby heroine's taste for cakes in *Washington Square* and says that he feels he should 'write it very small' – Proust is about Life. 'Oh, for heaven's sake!' you cry – 'not that old meaningless piece of vaporising . . . *Life*? Jesus! What the hell is *Life*? Can't you do any better than that? How long has it been since your adolescence?' Or: 'We haven't heard this sort of tosh since F. R. Leavis.'

But Life it is. We humans are, whatever else we may be, certainly conscious, experiencing beings. If our lives are anything they are that.[10] We aren't really the 'selves' we once thought we were, and we are almost certainly not 'souls'. We aren't prepared to identify ourselves as sociological statistics ('Hello! I'm a male C2 in a service industry working in the peri-urban south-east. Who are you?') nor just as

---

10 I am somewhat heartened in my interpretation by this comment from Ronald Hayman whose *Proust* of 1990 is one of the best biographies of the great novelist in English: 'In Proust's hands the novel became an attempt less to trap life between the pages of a book than to trap consciousness.' This seems a contradiction of my thesis except that for me 'life' is an unreal speculation whereas consciousness is life, or what we have really, instead of life. See the non-distinction between colander and cullender in the next footnote, no. 11, below for a comparison.

categories such as Parent, Schoolgirl, Marketing Executive, Sportsman, Sister, Musician or Old Person – sorry, Senior Citizen. And I notice that we are increasingly leery of being forced to identify our gender or our marital status. But we are certainly conscious, experiencing beings. Without conscious experience we are meat.

Politics, economics and sociology, which are not concerned with subjectivity, can't be the only important things then. So perhaps we should look at life again, try again, this time with the help of Proust, to see if we can find something else? Try again, fail again, fail better. We feel there to be 'something else' there in his prose, in every clause, shining at us sideways. It isn't only Proust who can produce this effect but he is the best example, and although other writers catch some of these 'other' things that I am trying to demonstrate, Proust does it best. Or at least at the greatest length.

So what is 'Combray' about? We come from reading it stuffed, *farci* with what might be called Life, certainly enough. But what is it made of? What *is* life? Here is an excerpt for us to see.

> How I loved it: how clearly I can see it still, our church at Combray! The old porch by which we went in, black, and full of holes as a cullender, was worn out of shape and deeply furrowed at the sides (as also was the holy water stoup to which it led us) just as if the gentle grazing touch of the cloaks of peasant-women going into the church, and of their fingers dipping into the water, had managed by agelong repetition to acquire a destructive force, to impress itself on the stone, to carve ruts in it like those made by cart-wheels upon stone gate-posts against which they are driven every day. Its memorial stones, beneath which the noble dust of the Abbots of Combray, who were

buried there, furnished the choir with a sort of spiritual pavement, were themselves no longer hard and lifeless matter, for time had softened and sweetened them, and had made them melt like honey and flow beyond their proper margins, either surging out in a milky, frothing wave, washing from its place a florid gothic capital, drowning the white violets of the marble floor; or else reabsorbed into their limits, contracting still further a crabbed Latin inscription, bringing a fresh touch of fantasy into the arrangement of its curtailed characters, closing together two letters of some word of which the rest were disproportionately scattered. Its windows were never so brilliant as on days when the sun scarcely shone, so that if it was dull outside you might be certain of fine weather in church. One of them was filled from top to bottom by a solitary figure, like the king on a playing-card, who lived up there beneath his canopy of stone, between earth and heaven; and in the blue light of its slanting shadow, on weekdays sometimes, at noon, when there was no service (at one of those rare moments when the airy, empty church, more human somehow and more luxurious with the sun shewing off all its rich furnishings, seemed to have almost a habitable air, like the hall–all sculptured stone and painted glass–of some mediaeval mansion), you might see Mme. Sazerat kneel for an instant, laying down on the chair beside her own a neatly corded parcel of little cakes which she had just bought at the baker's and was taking home for her luncheon. In another, a mountain of rosy snow, at whose foot a battle was being fought, seemed to have frozen the window also, which it swelled and distorted with its cloudy sleet, like a pane to which snowflakes have drifted and clung, but flakes illumined by a sunrise--the same, doubtless, which purpled the reredos of the altar with tints so fresh that they seemed rather to be thrown on it for a moment by a light shining from outside and shortly to be extinguished than painted and permanently fastened on the stone. And all of them were so old that you could see, here and there, their silvery antiquity sparkling with the dust of centuries and shewing in its threadbare brilliance the very cords of their lovely tapestry of glass. There was one among them which was a tall panel composed of a hundred little rectangular windows, of blue principally, like a great game of patience of the kind planned to beguile King Charles VI; but, either because a ray of sunlight had gleamed through it or because my own shifting vision had drawn across the window, whose colours died away and were rekindled by turns, a rare and transient fire– the next instant it had taken on all the iridescence of a peacock's tail, then shook and wavered in a flaming and fantastic shower, distilled and dropping from the groin of the dark and rocky vault down the moist walls, as though it were along the bed of some rainbow grotto of sinuous stalactites that I was following my parents, who marched before me, their prayer-books clasped in their hands; a moment later the little lozenge windows had put on the deep transparence, the unbreakable hardness of sapphires clustered on some enormous breastplate; but beyond which could be distinguished, dearer than all such treasures, a fleeting smile from the sun, which could be seen and felt as well here, in the blue and gentle flood in which it washed the masonry, as on the pavement of the Square or the straw of the market-place; and even on our first Sundays, when we came down before Easter, it would console me for the blackness and bareness of the earth outside by making burst into blossom, as in some springtime in old history among the heirs of Saint Louis, this dazzling and gilded carpet of forget-me-nots in glass.

In what sense is this *about life*? We can start to test that by asking another question: what are the things that this passage is *not* about? Well, it isn't for instance a description of a building that would be of much interest to a student of architecture and it doesn't really give the history of Combray church either. We are not being *informed* here, there are no politics or economics present, no *measurement*, and there is a feeling that these would be quite irrelevant if they were added; there is no judgement, no psychology, no sociology, no *assessment* of anything and no attempt to connect this passage to anything else in the novel or, indeed, to anything else in life as usually conceived. This is not an educational passage or a moral one; it leads to nothing; in a sense it means nothing, it has no function, not even a literary one. Above all, considering that it is a long description of a church, there is nothing whatsoever about religion here, no theology, no philosophy. It has no symbolic undertow; it cannot be *interpreted*. It consists of a presentation of the conscious experience of a particular boy in a particular place at a particular moment; it offers us the narrator's consciousness now, remembering his conscious experience then.

Each detail is in the narrator's awareness, not elsewhere. This, as we shall see throughout the novel, is him living. He experiences, as we all do all the time, not by brute perception but in a haze of observation and conscious comparison-making. Nothing leads to anything else beyond the comparison, nothing is concluded, all is present and immediate – like consciousness itself – like, as one might say, life itself. Thus the holes in the stonework of the porch make him think of a 'cullender',[11] presumably one he has seen in Françoise's kitchen on one of his many visits there.

---

11 Worried by this odd spelling chosen by the translator I consulted an online dictionary and discovered this very helpful explanation: 'As nouns the difference between **colander** and **cullender** is that colander is a bowl-shaped kitchen utensil with holes in it used for draining food such as pasta while **cullender** is a **colander**.'

But that is all. This isn't a symbol or part of some complex allegory; no judgement is passed on kitchen equipment or the employment of cooks; there is no suggestion that something in history or the narrator's life is, say, *draining away*. All that happens is that the boy's mind (read 'his experience of life', his consciousness of himself in the world) makes a connection. This is not a *Bildungsroman*.

We can't fail to notice the heavy presence in the passage of a lexical field concerning the past, specifically the Middle Ages, but we should again notice what Proust *doesn't* make of this. There are the cart wheels that have endlessly scraped the stone, 'agelong' repetitions, abbots and tombs and Latin; there are a couple of early French kings thrown in. But this is not about the past. This is only about the boy's perception and experience. Elsewhere the narrator discusses motor cars, Zeppelins and the latest fashions (or, as we say, 'Paris fashions') or discusses eating oysters, or being Jewish, or hotel bedrooms, or the tortures of jealousy, but the novel isn't *about* any of these. None of them stands up for a moment longer than it needs to in its demonstration of the only thing that happens in all the hundreds of pages. There appears to be no real plot, but then isn't it a very brave person who has anything very convincing to say about 'the plot' of his or her life? What is the *plot* of your life? The past is everywhere and determines our experience, we relate to it all the time, it makes things seem to us as they seem to us, it colours our perceptions. That's all. It isn't a *story*.[12]

Besides the past (here, as always, *present* of course) there is the sunlight and the things it does to the inside of

---

12 For a rather wonderful attack on the notion of life as a narrative see Galen Strawson's essay 'A Fallacy of Our Age' in *Things that Bother Me*, 2018.

the church. No conclusions whatever are to be drawn from this. The colours are not symbolic, the religious images have nothing to do with religion, Mme Sazerat's cakes do not 'represent' anything at all, the stained glass has no artistic or aesthetic significance. There is a lot of metaphor and simile, from the sunlight's 'smiling' to its 'throwing' or 'shewing' or 'shining' or 'flooding', but this isn't meant to build to any interpretation, it is simply how the narrator's mind works, as all of our minds work, by comparison and memory.

Perhaps Proust's novel is about the relationship between art and life, with art coming out on top? If so does it mean that *art* is our life? Or the meaning of our lives? This seems unlikely because his presentation of his life is so personal, so restricted to the narrator-as-boy, that we are confronted with a circularity if we try to read it as Aestheticism: yes, out of this huge description we see the young Marcel trying to connect some bits of his own life to art; but it is *his* life, not ours, not 'humanity's', not 'a bit of art'. No amount of historical knowledge about the stonework at the church or statistics concerning its construction and dimensions are worth a groat in comparison with the subjective reaction of the young Marcel to his local place of worship. Everything is subsumed in this writing, as in life itself, to the single primordial fact that he is conscious of a building, that he knows it and reacts to it as we do to our parents, our schools, the weather, a song or a kiss, through memory and imagination, consciously. Nothing we *know* about this in a rationalist sense matters a damn as we see, feel and react to these things. Experience (which is the reaction of consciousness to its surroundings) trumps analysis and explanation and the capturing of life in jars. This is not Enlightenment writing.

Here is another example of the life of a character in the novel. Françoise, the servant, cook, maid-of-all-work and faithful retainer to Marcel's family is of course a fictional character. In fact she is thus something that she herself at one point calls 'not a real person'. But the narrator is at pains to tell us that the first novelist who ever wrote came up with a wonderful trick: by putting imaginary people between the pages of a book he made them *more real not less*. For literary characters don't carry with them the irrelevancies of flesh and appearance or any necessary objective baggage, burdens forever shifting and forever standing between us and a comprehension of them, in the way that 'real people' do. Liberated from the heavy weight of physical existence and objective explanation, their subjectivity flowers in our imaginations – becoming thus *our* subjectivity – and they become clearer, more moving, cleaner, sharper.

In this way, more visibly than even our 'real' best friends, Françoise emerges to us as the humble, sadistic, loyal, illiterate, determined, strong-charactered, prejudiced woman whom the *reader* has only just met – say in 1950, or 1990, or today, right now a century after her creator's death, and presumably a century after her own fictional demise. She rises again, resurrected, standing in the sunshine that comes into her kitchen as she prepares another large and delicious meal for Marcel and his family.

With a wonderful trick of his own Proust lets Françoise demonstrate his point about how and where we actually live. The kitchen maid whom she torments that summer in Combray, forcing her to peel mountains of asparagus because she, the kitchen maid, is allergic to it and it makes her eyes and nose run, falls pregnant and goes into a very painful labour. While she sweats and groans the narrator's mother sends Françoise to fetch a book that describes various forms of pain and their remedies, but this errand seems to be taking a long time and the narrator, still a boy, is sent to look for the entirely unsympathetic Françoise. When he finds her it turns out that she has found the book in question and is reading it with her eyes full of tears. She emits her own groans as she learns of the sufferings of women in labour and looks up from the book in real distress but without any sense that she should be hurrying back to help the distress of her 'real' kitchen colleague. Her experience of the agonies of another person is internal, derived from a book, irrelevant to the experience of the poor kitchen maid. No external comment is made on this, no explanation offered; the scene closes without much more ado. Even in the most drastic circumstances, we have learnt, we experience what we experience and nothing else. Empathy on Françoise's part for a 'real person' would be something *made up*, a prescription from a realm that is closed to her.

This subjective-over-objective rule will apply throughout the novel, as throughout our own lives. Experience of the real Balbec will disappoint Marcel when he gets there, as will experience of the real Venice once he has visited it. The best play the theatres of Paris can put on will resemble Marcel's imagination of them in almost no way at all. Love, the aristocracy, friendship, military life, the beach, girls, all things bright and beautiful, all will fall before the sharp scythe of actual experience. If only we could live in the worlds of literature!

And then again the norms of our culture are also to blame. It is not only that reality fails to correspond to the clear lines of the imagination, it is also that our current notion of *actual experience* has itself been hijacked by the assumptions of another discourse; these are that objectivity, science, theory and the material will reveal reality to us.[13] The pattern thus goes as follows: a fictional kitchen maid in labour, or the fictional Françoise, or the imagined Venice are more real and more moving than any 'real' servant or city could be. This is because the 'real' servant or city come to us as actual experiences of a reality wrapped up in a number of unhelpful layers of thinking. When we examine or discuss that supposed reality we do so with the obtuse tools we have been given, the tools of objectivity, science and the material, and we fail to see.

***

Going out when the sun is shining in July, guiltily we try to experience a 'real' summer's day. We look about and try to make it *be* something or *mean* something, we try to capture it with our cameras or our imaginations, we point out its beauties to our companions: 'What a lovely day!' we say, and 'We must start having picnics – we must go to the beach!' We know the stories. But the day is lost. Objectivity, science and the material trump our lives in the shape of the demon Expectation. Watch:

We look at the grass in the fields that summer's day. It is dry, warm to the touch, fully there and needing no explanation. But we are condemned to see it in another light: for us it is only weakly and secondarily the grass we smell and touch; we know that primarily it is to be defined as a political and economic matter, or as a piece of botany or meteorology. It is not free to enter our minds in a more

---

[13] This is what Philip Goff will call 'Galileo's Error' in a book of that name, 2019.

properly subjective way; it is absent to us and so our own presence is compromised. We ask 'What is it?' and follow that up with other questions: 'What is grass?' 'What is this feeling?' 'Why do I feel it?' 'What does it mean?' And, of course, 'How can I capture it? Keep it? Or come back to it . . . but will it still be here, here *like this*?' Obviously not. Our Enlightenment minds destroy our connection to subjective reality.

Marcel's Françoise looks and smells and sounds herself in an identifiable way, though Proust never goes as far as giving her an external identity; she is the archetype of herself, complete and substantial. When she prepares dinner, serving her endless asparagus, making delicious chocolate puddings, they rise before us, perfect and immortal. But alas, with *our* education the first thing we are likely to think about Françoise is that she is a poor, exploited creature, a person who has had very little education herself and very few chances in life, a domestic servant in an unfair society. We think of the politics and economics of nineteenth-century France and we allow ourselves to sweep Françoise away as a victim, as someone leading a life that could not have been as full or as good as ours of course have been. She is to be smiled at (very reasonably in one way; she is often hilarious) but not taken seriously. Thus in a *trahison des clercs* we dismiss and let down the very people our political and economic theories were designed to help and protect.

But there is another way. Françoise has lived, and in the novel *lives*, a life in which her everyday reality is her experience, felt as precious by herself. Her out-dated opinions are as nothing compared to the sunlight in the garden at Combray, or her experience of preparing Tante Leonie's lunches, or her trudging to the shop where she pretends to make some small purchase in order to ask the knowledgeable shop-assistant some detail of town gossip to take back to Tante Leonie who lives on such titbits: Was Mme Goupil late for Mass? Did she get to the church before the Consecration? This, these *thoughts*, are Françoise's life, her experience in all its subjectivity, quite regardless of whether she is a member of an exploited servant class or has been denied her human rights. No political or economic change will improve those things without changing *her*. And who has the right to take upon themselves such a reformation? And why should they? And what if she doesn't want it?

Proust then shows us two things. That the world of the imagination is more real than the world around us[14], and that our experience of living in the world is intensely private, subjective and real when we are not distracted by the 'truths' of politics, economics, science and materialism. Françoise does not know that she does not know. *We* know, of course . . . allegedly. But what do we know? That there is something wrong with this woman? That she should not be as she is? That her experience is impoverished? These are the things our education, in its broad sense, has taught us. But are they true?

Objective truths are out there in black and white, of course; all the evidence of the material universe shows us that the cottage without sanitation is less healthy that the house with running water (statistics *à l'appui*), that our education is, up to a point, ipso facto better for 'us', for 'society', for 'people', for 'humanity' than the old ignorance

---

14 Elsewhere, when considering the paintings of Elstir, the narrator points out that 'things' only enter into their reality when they are really seen, seen that is through the eyes of art.

of the rural individual. We are entirely and unthinkingly convinced that paid holidays are or should be a *right* that all should have, that poverty is a bad thing, that a vote in an election is a means of creating happiness, that equality of opportunity is the only fair thing, that nobody should ever have to show deference to anybody else. So, naturally, the dweller in the tower block, struggling through polluting traffic morning and evening in order to stare at a computer screen at a place of 'work', a person whose values are substantially material, perhaps the characteristic modern man or woman . . . this person is clearly, obviously, to be envied by the likes of Françoise. Look at the progress we have made! How jealous she would be if she could see where we have got to! Our modern character can spend his or her evening on Facebook! How could anyone not envy that? How dreadful it must have felt to be without a fridge in those summers at Combray, without a car. How good these modern goods are for us. How happy they've made us. We unthinkingly think.

And we go on, worried if there is a quarter's dip in our rate of growth (three whole months of *not getting even richer* . . . yikes!), concerned about the 'provision' of everything: health, choice, freedom. But these things, even if they are good, do not determine personal experience, do not define consciousness.

7. Subjective and Experiential, or Objective and Experimental?

What is life like? Where can we find it and learn its secrets, open as they seem to be? Here is an attempt by Proust to convey an answer, the merest sketch of an answer, to these questions.

In *Du côté de chez Swann* the eponymous character, a Parisian socialite and millionaire living a life of ease in the 1860s, has fallen in love with Odette de Crécy, a lady no better than she should be as people used to say and certainly a coquette who, without being very clever, knows instinctively how to make men fall in love with her and knows how to torture them once they have fallen. Somewhat insensitive, in her egoism she doesn't really focus on hurting her men, it's just that she has to make a living out of her charms and a tormented amorous admirer is more likely to come up with those little five-thousand franc presents when she needs them than one who isn't in love with her. She may once have been a common prostitute, she may have had lesbian affairs, she is beginning to lose her looks, but Swann is deep in the travails of his love for her and his entire life is being slowly ruined by the irrational passion which dominates his every waking moment and some sleeping ones (but then, what would a rational passion be?).

Their love has been serenaded in the salon of Mme Verdurin by a few bars from a sonata for piano and violin composed by one Vinteuil. This acts as a leitmotif both for the reader and for these two characters and at first Odette shares Swann's excitement at hearing it every time they are at the Verdurins. But now Odette's love, which may perhaps have been a pretence from the start, has certainly cooled and Swann is in an ever-descending, Dantean spiral of agony (the literary comparison is Proust's) or in other words in a hell of jealousy and unrequited love.

Hanging about rather unwillingly at an afternoon concert in a private drawing room, wondering if Odette may show her face there (she won't of course) he suddenly realises that the piece of music being played is their special Vinteuil which then reaches the 'little phrase' that has been the national anthem of this, the great love affair of his life. Proust, monster paragraphist as he is, has been girding his loins for this moment. A mere 120 large pages have gone by since 'Un amour de Swann' began and now this quite old, quite ill and quite definitely tortured man is going to learn what love is like, and thus what his life is and has been. His climactic paragraph, first of a series of huge swoops of language that will end twenty-eight pages later with the astonishing confession from his own lips 'To say that I've ruined years of my life, that I have wanted to die, that I've had my great love, for a woman whom I didn't much like and who wasn't my type!' begins thus, as he hears the '*petite phrase*':

> But suddenly it was as if she [Odette] had entered the room [she hasn't, of course] and this apparition struck him with such a terrible pang of suffering that he had to put his hand up to his heart. The violin had risen to some high notes where it remained as if waiting for something

and which went on holding these notes because it, the violin, was at such a pitch of waiting that it could already see the approach of its object and was making a desperate effort to continue holding on until it [the object] arrived and to welcome it before it [the violin] expired, trying with all its strength to keep the path open so that it [the object] might come in, just as one holds open a door which, left to itself, will fall back automatically. And before Swann even had time to understand and to say to himself 'It's the little phrase from the sonata by Vinteuil; I won't listen to it!' all his memories of the time when Odette loved him, which he had until now managed to keep out of sight down in the depths of his being, fooled by this sudden ray of light from the time of true love that they [the memories] imagined had now returned, had woken up again to sing desperately to him with no pity for his present plight the forgotten songs of happiness.

This is a mere beginning. Swann, after two paragraphs comprising sixty-three dense lines in which he envisions a miserable figure which, as he takes a little time to realise, is in fact himself (*'C'était lui-même'*) returns to the music and, in a paragraph of over a hundred lines, considers the relationship between himself, Odette, music and love. It is an astonishing *tour de force*. It will continue, as we have seen, if somewhat more off than on, for a further twenty-five pages.

The point here is not to underline Proust's amazing abilities with language but rather to mark a contrast. For, just as the years of the narrator's childhood at Combray are held concealed in a little *madeleine* and a teaspoonful of *tisane* brought together for a few seconds, so the five or six crucial notes in the Vinteuil sonata contain within themselves vast tracts of time, of emotion, of Swann's life in all its subjective intensity. And, paradoxically, if we want to unpack that, to come a little closer to any sort of understanding of that life, of that experience, we need not just some tea and a small cake but thousands of words that seem, for all their complexity and elegance, a mere beginning, a few feeble gestures towards understanding what a lived experience is actually like. The novel really should be a lot longer.

Now let us go the other way. To a university no less, to the libraries, to the internet. What can we find there about this sort of event? There are, for a start, musicological studies and histories of music that will explain the sonata form and its development including technical commentary on composition, keys, progressions, dynamics and so on; all very laudable. And then there is a sociology of love which might help to explain why Swann can't simply marry the woman he loves (though he does in the end); and we will find psychological studies explaining the mentality of the later-nineteenth century with its obsessions and anxieties. Then there is the more general history of the period Proust is writing about, which can be very good but which must always remain on the objective surface. There is Freud, there is biology, and there are statistics about all this. In fact, there is the whole intellectual panoply, quite neatly divided into the departments of institutions such as universities, which are our legacy from the Enlightenment and its successors in the nineteenth and twentieth centuries.

Here we have *explanation*, writ large and long, and *analysis* and all the thinking about love, about sexual relations, about the mythologies of class and convention that can be studied. It is the lifeblood of our publications, the norm by which we think, the only, surely the only way to go, our legacy from the Enlightenment. But does any of this, *any of it at all*, touch the matter of Swann's subjectivity, of your or my actual experience? Can these objective sciences capture or make *any* useful comments about the subjective moment?

Let us imagine that we have invented a perfect explanation, a definitive analysis and assessment of love. Our greatest scholars, let us say, have provided us with compendious explanatory volumes covering every aspect of what is happening to Swann, or to you or indeed me; we have learnt the physiology, psychology and sociology of the gift or affliction that is the Divine Passion; we know its history (having perhaps read Dennis de Rougemont's *Love in the Western World*) and its usual pathways. To all intents and purposes we know about love. But none of that goes very far with the individual in love. It is rather like explaining an incurable cancer to the victim or the victim's family. 'Yes, yes' they will say, 'Thank you for explaining,' but their life will not be in that reply; their life will be in the immediate consciousness of pain, of fear perhaps, of your kindness or abruptness, of what they were reading before you came in, of the mud on your shoes, of the nurse in the hallway, of death behind her. Their life will be going on as though what you have said is in some deep way irrelevant. And indeed at one level none of it matters just as nothing in Proust's description of the church at Combray matters or means anything more than 'this is what I saw and heard and felt and thought – *mon expérience, quoi?*'

One can't collect life. It isn't like seashells or flowers or money or the books you have read on the Byzantine Empire. These you can multiply, life you can't. *Pace* Sartre ('authentic existence') or Camus ('more life') or Saint Paul ('life more abundant') there is nothing you can *do* with 'life'. Milo Minderbinder and a chum of his in *Catch 22* have a self-imposed programme of life-prolongation which includes sitting through the most boring lectures they can find (and this is the armed forces we're talking about) because during them time will slow down. Hilarious but, alas, a doomed enterprise. One speaks of 'my life' or 'her life', and that's perfectly useful for everyday purposes, but it stands as Newton's scheme of reality to Einstein's. The physics of the *Principia* works all right for the everyday, but the facts presented by his successor contradict it. So with 'my life': I don't increase it by understanding it better, for in truth I don't *have* a life and it anyway isn't the sort of thing that can be increased. I simply go on, following the Tao. Not even that.

I tend to imagine that my life has something to do with my self, or my 'Self'; but there again, look carefully and you'll see that, although it's useful to refer to yourself as yourself when going about your normal affairs, you don't actually have a self. You go through time as a consciousness, not as a bag of collected minutes and hours. You experience whatever comes to you with your currently-available ideas and memories and you look back on whatever it was as irretrievably lost. But in truth it was never really found, got, possessed, had. You know that you are always waiting (Pascal: 'Man is always preparing to be happy; it is therefore inevitable that he never is so') and while waiting you can imagine a satisfactory future at some other time, a paradise to be gained. And you could also be aware of Proust's dictum: '*Les vrais paradis sont les paradis que l'on a perdu.*'

Swann's experience of Vinteuil's music is a monster version of all of our experiences all of the time. But perhaps we have forgotten experience itself as a category in our rush to reform and improve everything around us in our lives and societies. Serious discussion seems now to be limited to politics, economics and sociology. When did you last participate in a serious discussion of religion or poetry or silence or pain or colour at the dinner table? Who has got heated, when sitting next to you, about the inner sense of flow generated by watching water or the sense of happiness that a small boy may feel at a favourite moment in a book you are reading to him? What do we ever say about our real experiences? We sneer at the Victorians for their prudery about certain well-known topics concerning the body and its functions, but you can shock or disgust modern people just as easily by dwelling on, say, your jealousy or your fear of death, and I don't mean *Jealousy or Fear of Death* – I mean *your experience of them* of course. As Proust demonstrates, there is a very great deal that can be said about these things from a subjective point of view. But we are not encouraged to say it.

8. Happiness

In his 1888 essay 'The Dorsetshire Labourer' Thomas Hardy expressed the opinion that happiness would 'find her last true refuge on earth' among the Wessex peasants he had known in his childhood. This must give us pause.

It is a cliché of Victorian sociology that the Dorset workfolk (as Hardy often called farm labourers, sticking to his Anglo-Saxon roots) were the worst off of all of England's agricultural hands. They lived in the county which had the worst rural 'deprivation', a fact which perhaps explains why it was in Dorset that farm workers made the first attempt to band together to improve their lot when the 'Tolpuddle Martyrs' formed an early trades union in 1833. Their action was a then-illegal protest against what we would now call their 'pay and conditions' and it aroused considerable sympathy. Sentenced to transportation to Australia in 1834 they were pardoned in 1836 and returned to England in the years that followed. Yet it was, amazingly, among such people that Hardy found that true happiness seemed to persist; not his own happiness – that would have taken a very different sort of performance by the Purblind Doomsters who ruled his universe – but the happiness of the good-natured poor, the cheerfully exploited and ignorant; and the simple joy of the possessionless and powerless.

What can this possibly mean? Was it a Christian *contemptu mundi* – luxury is an evil, the world's treasure is nothing? Surely not. Was it Buddhist detachment that he found in his 'Rustic Chorus', among the Joseph Poorgrasses and Christian Cantles of his novels?[15] Hardy saw his humble workfolk as people untroubled by the developments of the modern world and untroubled by excessive desire – so perhaps a little Buddhist. The sure way into trouble, anguish and neurosis, Hardy came to see increasingly as he aged, was by engaging in any confrontation with the modern and any involvement in the powerful machinery of love. Between them these will destroy Farmer Boldwood, Eustacia Vye, Michael Henchard, Giles Winterborne and of course Tess Durbeyfield and Jude Fawley, not to mention a number of lesser characters. But the very least of his characters, the people whose sights are set at the humblest level, the Marty Souths and Suke Damsons, the Mark Clarks, Abel Whittles and Cainey Balls, some of them virtual simpletons, are so far below the purview of the vengeful gods that they are let alone by fate and can make their way quite peacefully along the cool sequester'd vale of life. They are not 'happy', of course, but they do have some happiness and they do avoid the worst horrors, which is about as near to actual happiness as Hardy can see any of us getting.

And what, besides that vague possession, did they have? Very little on the material plane, and on the intellectual or spiritual plane nothing more than a sketchy version of Anglican Christianity which meant that they went to church, respected the vicar (more or less) and considered that 'the sky folk' had a plan for them with which they hardly needed to trouble themselves. They enjoyed a light-

---

15 Jagdish Dave thinks so in this Hindu-Buddhist reading of Hardy, *The Human Predicament in the Novels of Thomas Hardy* of 1990.

hearted respect for the squirearchy and those set above them along with a preference for beer and sunny weather. Joseph Poorgrass's inability to find the right Epistle for the Sunday service (he is church clerk) leads him to complain that his New Testament has tricked him and that, instead of containing the reading he is looking for, it is full of 'nothing but danged Ephesians'. The humour belongs, one suspects, as much to Joseph's original as to Thomas Hardy; and he doesn't care deeply about very much, for all his 'Scripture manner'. And Widow Edlin, in one of the darkest parts of *Jude the Obscure*, can't quite tell why people are making all this fuss about love and marriage. Her protests are simple and eloquent: 'Weddings be funerals nowadays I believe,' she says, and remarks that when she got married in the old days people thought of marriage 'No more than o' a game o' dibs.'

But this life, passed quietly year after rural year, punctuated by the holidays and the feasts of the church and laid out in the inexorable routine labour of the four seasons, culminating in Harvest Home and Christmas and punctuated by Easter, Whitsun, the haymaking and the sheep washing, seems to satisfy some deep ancestral need in this 'rustic chorus' who observe the tragedies of the novels from a slight distance. Educated they are not, and imaginative only rarely, but they are kind, good-hearted and stoical, incapable of a harsh word. Not one of them is a villain. When Gabriel Oak comes among them there is no resentment of his superiority and the only advice they give him is when they drop his bacon sandwich into the ashes and it comes out gritty: 'Don't 'ee chaw quite close master shepherd' they counsel, concerned for his teeth. You can see how amenable and pliant they are faced with the slings and arrows of outrageous fortune.

They had enough to eat, just. They calculated that their miserable wages were so small that there was no point in trying to save for old age – the workhouse was their inevitable destination at the end of their lives – but they took such things philosophically and in general didn't think very much about death or, as we have seen, about marriage or success in life, let alone advancement or change. The superior types among them, the Clym Yeobrights and Judes and Tesses head straight out into the bigger world looking for disaster and finding it, while the lower section of rural society, not expecting much and getting little, have no illusions about their fate and accept it.

It is tempting to compare this image of the Dorset workfolk with Tolkien's picture of his hobbits. They too are rustic and simple, local and without great ambition; agricultural work and innocent pleasures involving singing, tobacco and beer fill their lives and they live in a world almost entirely without crime. It is, of course, a world of childlike, even childish purity of heart, a world quite impossible in what we currently call 'reality', unimaginable in practice and clearly in serious denial about disease, death and personal strife. An idyll, a fantasy.

But my point about such groups as Hardy's peasants and the hobbits is not that our world could ever be brought to resemble their world, and in many ways it is better that it doesn't, or even that their world was necessarily idyllic, but that we humans have a strong taste for that sort of world, a suspiciously strong taste, and it is this taste that needs addressing for it is ubiquitously present among us and is perhaps not taken seriously.

Tourists, people looking for houses to buy, advertising agencies, the illustrators of children's books, millionaires, hotel websites and many other people involved in business situations all the world over reveal an amazingly uniform series of preferences: a preference for the small over the big, the local over the international, the cute over the monstrous, the natural over the artificial, the quiet over the strident, the rural over the urban and the modest over the proud. One could greatly extend this series of antonyms, but my list is enough to show how we have here a well-known semantic field that everyone in the modern world can recognise. In this semantic field lie: peace, things that are human-scale, wooden objects, quiet streams, simple lives, villages, country churches, meadows, polite children, soft voices, unspoilt valleys, flowers, kindness, gentler kinds of music, the traditional feminine, meditation, twilight, the scent of honeysuckle, monastic chanting, old buildings . . . and I could go on. From Chaucer's description of a spring day to the backgrounds in Walt Disney's cartoons and on to television series such as *Game of Thrones* there is a range of basic images, tropes and touching scenes that have been endlessly repeated in the ever-more-frequently-presented plethora of pictures that dominates our lives. It's largely the product of Western culture but it seems to work internationally. Disney is global; Tolkien is universal.

You will have noticed that the photographs of houses for sale used on estate agents' websites tend to be misleading. The house is taken from the best angle, the one that excludes the big tin shed next door or the block of council flats at the bottom of the garden; much stress is laid on quaint nooks in house and garden and on 'period features' while the sound of the nearby motorway remains unmentioned. Similarly very few people pay money to visit Milton Keynes or Port Talbot or Livingston unless they have to. Why not? These places aren't *that* bad in terms of 'liveability' and they aren't terribly crowded or dirty. Ah! But they have no 'soul', no 'heart', no 'organic' structure, no depth, no age, no 'natural' *je ne sais quoi* that would make them homely or comfortable or able to touch your heart. You can't imagine getting a lump in your throat as you think about them during a period of exile. Equally pubs, even if they are in squalid areas of concrete and glass, often attempt to recreate an 'olde worlde' feeling and atmosphere.

There is cognitive dissonance here. We will buy a house because the adjective 'Georgian' has been added to the mention of its 'up-and-over garage doors' (I have actually seen this) or because there is 'a trout-stream' going through the garden (again, a real example; the estate agent when challenged insisted that 'trout *have* been sighted'). But what are we paying that extra money for? I have seen villages ruined by a crowd of soulless houses that have been added to their nice old centres by developers who announce on a large billboard at the entrance to their lamentable 'estate' 'Come and Live in X! The Conservation Village!' Even when buying a jerry-built box in 2020 we are suckers for 'conserving' the special quality that that very box is destroying.

What is the psychology here? What do we *want*? I would suggest that we want to touch the hem of the garment of one of Hardy's workfolk to see if some of his or her happiness (or do I mean 'enlightenment'?) will rub off on us.

Happiness, the Buddha saw, lies not the fulfilment of desire but in its defeat. Alarmingly he suggests that we should detach ourselves not only from our pain and suffering but also from our pleasure and contentment. The stoical 'equal mind' is the way to go forward in life. Like Hardy's peasants, Buddhist monks when they express any affect at all tend to laugh. For the enlightened mind it is the only reaction left – humour separates people from the immediate pressure of the good and the bad, that is from desire or fear.

Behind detachment of this kind lies the absent self. It is all 'an illusion' in the sense that 'I' am not here, not now, not really; but it is always 'I' when I look. And everything else is impermanent too. So the only permanent thing is a thing that isn't there – the absent self. Happiness is rising above all the things that make you happy – or sad. For in the universe there seem to be two sorts of thing – one is the 'ten thousand things' of Buddhism, and the other is the subjectivity we oppose to them and can, with a huge effort, sometimes, see through them with. Only when we see that the latter must, inevitably, trump the former can we be free.

Of course our subjectivity only needs to be considered as 'nothing' in opposition to the many things of the universe. At another level, by another analysis, it is more like a sort of *nothing/something*. The word *nirvana* is related to the English word 'fan' – a blowing device – and begins with the well-known 'n' of negation found in Indo-European languages. So *nirvana* is what has been 'blown out'. The candle was there, the world was all around us but it is we who light it up with our consciousnesses and it's we who can extinguish it. That will be, and can be today in the right meditative state, the real enlightenment. The reverse of the thin paper on which life is written, its non-material side, is where happiness lies. We know this.

9. The Priesthood of Science

As Philip Goff has recently told us in his *Galileo's Error* of 2019, the Renaissance, the very thing that made the Enlightenment possible, began a revolution which did very well in removing what went before, namely unscientific thinking. But this revolution, usually referred to as 'the Rise of Science', didn't create the necessary conditions for a perfect replacement – no revolution ever does. Galileo's 'error' was to suggest that measurement, mathematics, science and the material are the only way we can approach an understanding of the universe, to the exclusion of all other ways. The result of this will be the application of rational thought to all areas of existence, a method confirmed in the eighteenth century as the only circus worth attending in our intellectual town. Locke and Newton at the end of the seventeenth century appeared to confirm the Galileo–Bacon programme and by the time Kant was using '*Aufklärung*' for the first time in this context in 1784 the die is cast – thinking can only go one way. Reading T. H. Huxley's essays a further century on in the 1870s we feel the victorious battle continuing; his lectures on the need for scientific and material solutions are sermons, rhetorical flights that most convincingly demonstrate that the answer to cholera epidemics or to the risk of fire in London is not prayer but practical, rational, scientific steps that we can take to prevent such catastrophes.

And right up until today the 'error' persists. Huge advances in medicine and engineering, and now in information technology, would seem to have vindicated the Galileo–Bacon programme, and our respect for scientists, doctors and rationalist experts in all fields has risen in direct proportion to these successes. Surgeons were once ranked with barbers; now they are the demi-gods of our hospitals. Rupert Sheldrake, himself a scientist of no mean order and a firm believer in science, calls this the establishment of a 'priesthood of science' – the unconscious development of a belief-system that is entirely material. Voltaire, in his excitement at reading Newton, declared himself to be an adherent of '*la religion newtonienne*'.[16]

This religion has a series of tenets that seem to most people today to be common sense. They include: a commitment to the material and its exploration and domination; this leads directly to the desirability of economic progress and ever-increasing 'growth'; and a responsibility on those in power to ensure high material living standards for the whole population; and thus the imperative need for ever-improving health, social care and even ordinary fitness. These are seen as the duty of governments and, indeed, as the 'right' of everyone on the planet. If this makes you think of that most Enlightenment of all documents, the American Constitution, you are on the proper track: its list of 'rights' famously starts with the right to 'life, liberty and the pursuit of happiness'. Of these the first is more or less self-evident

---

16 Not just Voltaire. The logical positivists of the 1920s and 1930s proclaimed their intention of replacing all forms of thinking, including political and social, with a materialist philosophy. They saw themselves as the inheritors of Locke and Hume and supported the Copenhagen Interpretation of quantum physics which dismisses the real existence of the unobservable.

(unless you happen to be visiting a death-row prisoner in Texas), the second provokes the question 'Whose liberty?' as, after all, your liberty to make money may conflict with my right not to be exploited, and the third gets us back to the economy, either directly through the dubious proposition that money buys happiness, or indirectly through the idea that those with money can pay taxes, taxes pay for medicine and education, for instance, and these increase the general happiness.

This religion, as befits its status as a materialist cult, is a religion of the body. 'Being good' is now equated not with the old-fashioned virtues but with not eating too much, with taking exercise, or with 'being good to yourself', a notable variation on the Christian injunction to 'do good to others'. It means having physical treats such as a holiday, a spa day, time off to relax and meditate or a nice meal. It looks in fact as if the two meanings of 'materialism' have been silently conflated: the philosophy underpinning science is, precisely, a scientific materialism while a materialistic approach to life is the underpinning of the consumer society.

Instead of 'God' the religion of science proposes the universe or nature as the last word, and instead of 'Providence' it proposes universal laws that cannot be altered. Instead of 'Charity' our new religion, being closely allied to the humanism that was born along with the science, offers its believers the means of bringing about a general amelioration of the lot of mankind. In this context the existence of 'charity shops' is intriguing; we feel guilty about throwing away material possessions that still have some value and thus feel impelled to pass them on to others in a way that salves our consciences *first* about the 'waste' of the objects concerned and only *secondly* about the way the profits will be given to a Good Cause.

Instead of 'Heaven' the religion of science suggests longer lives for ourselves and a better world for our grandchildren. It has in fact not moved very far, philosophically speaking, from its roots in eighteenth-century deism – we have to remember that both Hume and Voltaire considered themselves to be deists. The absent 'clock-maker' God of the Newtonian universe – resurrected many times and most effectively by William Paley in his *Natural Theology* of 1804 ('Paley's Evidences'), a set text in the university study of divinity until the 1920s – expresses himself in a series of laws and arrangements that hold for all time and are for the good of humanity and the planet in general. Modern materialism of course has removed the element of 'intelligence' from this early version of intelligent design but the resulting picture of the universe belongs to the same family as Paley's view of nature.

The religion of science then, child of the Enlightenment, is optimistic but exclusive. It promises much and predicts much – space travel, a cure for cancer – and is ready to step forward to help solve crises and natural catastrophes from drought in the Sahel to the coronavirus; its optimism lies in the claim that things will get better, that 'we can fix it', which itself is a faith parallel to the meliorist position of George Eliot and Thomas Hardy. More power, one has to say, to this one of its elbows; but its other elbow, the elbow of exclusivity, is sharper. With this elbow it defends itself from anything non-materialist and is famously intolerant of what it sees as aberrant opinions or what it is likely to call 'Woo-Woo'. Here we find Rupert Sheldrake's TED talk being banned[17] and Richard Dawkins refusing to look at Sheldrake's evidence for certain paranormal phenomena – literally refusing to look.

The priesthood of science has done much, but it has also resisted some interesting and possibly good things in a most unhelpful way. Apart from threatening the jobs of certain more open-minded medical and academic personnel, hard-line materialism has shown very little interest in such things as healing and the near-death experience evidence. The former promises a new sort of alleviation of human suffering, and in fact is now being used in some hospitals. St Thomas's in London was I think the first UK hospital to employ healers to relieve the pain of terminal cases in some children's wards. And if you would like to reduce your fear of death or your grief for a deceased relative there are few better ways of doing it than reading, or watching online, the stories of those who have been on the brink of death, had the most wonderful experience of their lives, been told it isn't their time to die, and come back, often against all the medical odds, to tell us about it.

My criticism of our new religion ignores, I admit, the honourable minority who constitute a resistance to

---

17 Rupert gave a talk entitled 'The Science Delusion' at TEDx Whitechapel, 12 Jan. 2013. The theme for the night was 'Visions for Transition: Challenging existing paradigms and redefining values (for a more beautiful world)'. In response to protests from two hardcore materialists in the US, the talk was taken out of circulation by TED, relegated to a corner of their website and stamped with a warning label. Room for discussion was made, but those who condemned the talk never showed up. The vast majority of those who spoke out were outraged, including those who'd never heard of morphic resonance. Ironically, before the banning the video had a modest 35,000 views; since then its clones have been watched over five million times. It's also been dubbed into Russian and has subtitles in 20+ languages.

mainstream thinking. Since the 1960s 'New Age' religion and an interest in Eastern imports such as meditation and yoga, alongside a much greater concern about what materialism is doing to the planet, have flourished at least in the thinking of this minority. In practice the situation is nonetheless rather gloomy. I picture even well-intentioned people who say and think the right open-minded things but who nonetheless drive to yoga classes in large cars and work enthusiastically in the sterile world of finance. That is a caricature, comparable to an accusation of champagne socialism, but in both cases it is noticeable that the headlong rush towards ever greater investment in the material (whether for the individual or society) shows no sign of abating.

The intellectual legerdemain that has been practised on us is that of all religions: we can call it the 'illusion of omniscience'. Orthodox Muslims, for instance, believe that theirs is the final religion, the overriding truth. They aspire both peacefully and less peacefully to the establishment of God's kingdom upon earth and are expected to think that their book is the last book, the complete book beyond which no other is really needed. Fundamentalist Christians are inclined to take the same attitude towards that other book that Muslims consider to be the predecessor to theirs – the Bible ('The Book').

Similarly with our religion of science. It has no single book but instead a near-infinity of books, articles, reports, lectures, theories and so on that aspire to be the book of nature. So prestigious is this myriad-headed volume that all other aspects of our lives are in danger of being taken over by it. Thus for our communal life we have sociology, the science of society, and for our personal lives psychology, the science of the mind. For politics we have economics and opinion polls, for philosophy we have semiotics, epistemology and symbolic logic. And behind all these lie the truths that we all believe: statistics, expert opinions, the latest research.

This religion has been responsible for a downgrading, in both the intellectual and non-intellectual worlds of our times, of the other sort of enlightenment. What is lacking from it is any serious recognition of consciousness, experience, life as lived by the perceiving subject and all those things that are not just the body, not the economy, not political. What is lacking is what can be (embarrassingly?) summarised as 'the spiritual', but even without that step there remain some awkward questions for this materialism such as How did mind arise from matter? What is consciousness? Questions the more urgent as it now seems that some people, sometimes, continue to be conscious after the doctors have declared them dead.

It has been estimated that there have been some twenty million near-death experience accounts recorded since Raymond Moody invented a name for these phenomena in 1975. In all of these, many of them demonstrably not false or fraudulent, the consciousness of the dying person leaves his or her body (an example of the out-of-body experience) and has a series of encounters that are now familiar, with dark tunnels, attractive lights, spirit beings and deceased relatives, before being told that it is 'not their time' and finding themselves back where they were, on the operating table for instance. In no other field would the science community overlook or ignore twenty million exceptional and very marking events reported, often enough, by medical staff.[18] NDE accounts are anathema to the religion

---

18 See, for instance, Pim van Lommel's *Universal Consciousness* of 2004.

of science, of course, but it is beginning to look as if the scientists who won't look at the evidence rather resemble the cardinals who wouldn't look through Galileo's telescope.

10. 'And is that all?'

The story is told of a young American and his reaction to reading *Middlemarch* when it first appeared. George Eliot's novel was published in book form in 1873 and it has been in print ever since. Virginia Woolf once said that 'all novels would be *Middlemarch* if they could'. So we can put it down as a well-known, heavyweight text for the Victorians and also for us today. It is thought of as highly intelligent, perceptive, amusing, accurate, moral, sensible and many other good things. But this young American: he rose from his chair when he had finished the last page of the great work *with tears in his eyes* and proclaimed to the heavens 'And is that all?' Possibly even 'My God! And is that all?'

Someone who has turned the pages of Eliot's humane and insightful work usually finds the story of this reaction surprising. Eliot is so warm, so funny! Life really does seem to go in the way she says and, after all, her novel isn't a *tragedy*. Indeed not. One might have tears in one's eyes when one has just finished reading *King Lear* ('*Enter King Lear with Cordelia dead in his arms*' does it for most people) but not *Middlemarch*, surely?

But in Eliot we are looking at the reaction of a sensitive mind to the famous 'disenchantment' of the world. This process was started by the Reformation, accelerated by the Enlightenment, resisted by romanticism and nineteenth-century medievalism, given a great boost by the Industrial

Revolution, renewed by modernism (and the modern in general) and finally completed by the two world wars, logical positivism, communism, Auschwitz and the materialist religion of today.

Our young American found no fairies in Eliot, no happy endings, no triumph, no extra weight put into the scales on the side of the good, no romantic heroines. Thus there is for a start Dorothea Brooke who wastes herself in a horrible marriage because she thinks that in the dry old duffer Casaubon she has found a sort of equivalent of her idea of Milton, someone she can sacrifice herself to nobly for the cause of religion and some other more vaguely conceived advantages. Then there is Rosamond Vincy who believes that by marrying the nice-looking nephew of a baronet she will be promoted from the comfortable dullness of urban middle-class life to the heavenly regions of the aristocracy, wrongly of course.

Both young ladies are to be bitterly disappointed. But far worse from the point of view of our American friend must have been the fates of the heroes, the intelligent medical idealist Tertius Lydgate and the charming and efficient Will Ladislaw. Neither of them comes to anything much at all in spite of their structurally heroic status and good looks, and they go to their insignificant fates in spite of very good intentions and their proven ability to overcome serious difficulties rather well. Dorothea and Rosamond are fools, each in her different way (or victims of poor education and unrealistic social ideals) but Tertius and Will do not have that disadvantage – their lives just happen to miss some of the better possibilities offered and they are just a bit unlucky. Their looks, their talents, their nobility do not mean, even though this is a *novel*, that they will get any 'appropriate' rewards. Eventually, with Dorothea's money and backing, Will does get into Parliament but it is almost a footnote when it occurs in a late chapter.

A little before that, in Chapter 80, we find an attitude we might call stoical. In the most mundane of all moments – a morning scene in which a labourer and his wife are watched by Dorothea as they make their way to work – the narrator/George Eliot mentions how we have all to wake up to 'labour and endurance' – nothing else is offered, certainly no transcendence of any kind. The quotation is well known: 'Far off in the bending sky was the pearly light; and she felt the largeness of the world and the manifold wakings of men to labour and endurance.'

The optimistic light here is, alas, only light, a mere meteorological phenomenon; it is hardly symbolic of anything at all except, perhaps, that a nice day may follow – though the sky is 'bending' and it *is* 'far off'.

David Hume suggested that we should 'cease to enquire, or cease to believe'. But we are not able as a species to do the former; we cannot stop *enquiring* and exploring. The Naked Ape has no choice but to go on trying to reduce the power of his predators and the threats of his environment, and he must find ever more ways to fulfil the desires planted in him by millions of years of evolution; worse, these desires become more complicated as history goes on, so his intelligence is pushed to find more sophisticated solutions, ones which have increasing potential to make humans unhappier as well as safer and, of course, to wipe humanity out as well as, just possibly, to save it.

As to the latter, *believing* is always believing in something that is other, something beyond, usually something better, some sort of *reward* here or hereafter. Discovering that the basic system of fiction – 'the good end happily, the bad unhappily . . . that is what fiction means' as the governess says in *The Importance of Being Earnest* – is merely fictional indeed, that there may not be much in the way of post-mortem compensation for suffering, and that the paradise on Earth proposed by communism turned out to be the gulag and the killing fields, these are reasons to weep for the sensitive soul who has been *believing* and is now beginning to *enquire*.

But is George Eliot's vision entirely without hope? Has she not just spent eight hundred pages lovingly and carefully painting episodes in the lives of people in whom we are interested? Have we not enjoyed *Middlemarch*? Is there not a satisfaction in having ourselves spent so long in the company of the inhabitants of the novel? Have we not learned lessons that are valuable? Have we not laughed?

She herself offered some ways forward in her modified positivism: her poem 'The Choir Invisible' asks (though to whom does it send its prayer?) that she be allowed to join the invisible choir of those who *make the world a better place*. I apologise for that cliché, much used in funeral eulogies, but it catches exactly what her verses say. This ambition puts her centrally in the highroad of Enlightenment optimism and the Whig interpretation of history. Your sacrifices have not been in vain – humanity will 'rise on the stepping stones of its dead selves to higher things' – as Tennyson had so beautifully, and vaguely, put it. Is this not enough?

But we now know that this is not enough, that humanity needs something more and that, against all the odds and the full official doctrine of the religion of science, there does seem to be something more. This something, which we would be well advised to become aware of, is precisely awareness. The disenchantment of the world has left us without gods, without magic, without wild places for the imagination or for a romantic visit, without strange peoples and exciting customs, without *older* ways of being . . . and none of these things is going to come back. We have exchanged enchantment for comfort, material prosperity, the advancement of science and the material magic of 'the wonders of nature'. One can feel the loss, and perhaps the gain, in our great interest in travel (reduced for the most part to holidays) and in our fascination with nature programmes on film and television. I have only to mention David Attenborough's series to make the point. Technology has permitted us to have intimate insights into things in nature that only a few years ago we could never have hoped to encounter in our ordinary lives: the deeps of the sea, the lives of snow leopards, the courtships of insects. We gasp at this as we do at the results of the exploration of space and the complexity and cunning of the latest medical apparatus. This is what we find 'wonderful!'

But, wonderful as it indeed is, is it *all*? If that is the question we feel impelled to ask there is only one way we can go. To employ one of the best-known clichés of spiritual teachers, we need to go *inside*.

The problem that will drive us *inside* presents itself with a sort of inexorable and depressing insistence when we find ourselves using the verb 'to have'. The amazing nature programmes on television give us much, but they don't give us anything we can feel we *possess*; there is a supplement of disquiet that may start with the feeling 'I'd love to go *there*! I'd like to see *that*!' and this might lead to some effort on our part to go *there* really and truly and to see *that*, but what would it amount to in the end? Probably it would be disappointing (have you tried getting deep into the Himalayas and waiting silently for days under canvas for a glimpse of a snow leopard?) and certainly it would be unsatisfying, as if we had been cheated in some way. In any event we would not feel that we had quite *possessed* the mountains or the animals in the way we hoped, we couldn't really say that we had *had* them.

For in truth possession is not one of life's long suits. Erich Fromm made this point very well in his *To Have and To Be*, a book of its time (1976) which suggested that humanity can choose between a focus on *having* or a focus on what we would now call 'experiences' or '*being*'. Possessing has had a good run for its money, appropriately enough, but it has not delivered everything we hoped. We too feel the force of the question 'And is that all?' And, as I say, there is only one way to go if we are ever to find anything else. Anything beyond the immediately material. And it is inside.

11. The Religion of Social Justice

Turning to the 'inside' as I suggested we do at the end of the last essay is essentially a religious gesture and one which fits nicely with the old religions, notably Buddhism and Christianity with their respective traditions of meditation and soul-searching. But 'going within' hardly fits with the new creed of our times, which I would call the religion of social justice – an expression meant to be equivalent to the normal definition of Christianity as the religion of love. Followers of Jesus have not always been loving and their codes and actions have often been rather remotely connected to the idea of charity, of course. As a good Catholic boy I thought it was important not to eat meat on Fridays and not to talk loudly in church, beliefs neither really offensive nor inoffensive in themselves but surely not ones that were much concerned with love. However, it remains the case that the core of the Christian religion is usually taken to be the love of one's neighbour.

It may help us to focus on the new creed if we look at its most symbolic and often most frequent expression, something close to its heart: the difficult question of race. The rabbi asked Jesus, 'Who is my neighbour?' and got the Good Samaritan as an answer. If you ask 'What is social justice?' you might well get 'the opposite of racism' as an answer.

During the world-wide anti-racist disturbances following the killing of George Floyd in June 2020 the following sentence appeared on the BBC website: 'England and Manchester City forward Raheem Sterling has backed protests taking place across the UK, saying "The only disease right now is the racism that we are fighting."' Sterling is an England footballer whose rhetorical choice caught our attention in a way he surely intended: racism is so bad, he appeared to say, and in particular so widespread across the globe, that it is worse than the coronavirus that at this point had killed more than 400,000 people. Arguing about which of these two things, the virus or racism, is the worse 'disease' would lead us into statistical quicksand from which there would be no exit ('How many incidents of racial abuse equate to one death?' 'How many black deaths equate to a thousand corona fatalities?'– that sort of thing) and isn't the point. The point of the hyperbole Sterling used is shown in the way his surprising comparison was taken: what we understood was 'We are all worried sick about the coronavirus, but you could say that this racism is *even worse*.' Nobody imagined for a moment that he intended to downplay the corona crisis; everyone recognised that he was making some such rhetorical claim as: 'Look, racism is so bad that even in these times of rampant and fatal pandemic there is something less obvious but which could actually be worse.' And he went on to make the comparison explicit but then neatly moderated his headline-catching first statement when he added, '*Just like* the pandemic, we want to find a solution to stop it.' Suddenly the rhetorical became the practical, for we do most certainly want to find a solution, to stop 'the spread' of the virus and also of the widespread problem of race.

Raheem Sterling's command of the sound-bite was perfect: hit hard with the first punch and then back off a little. Make them think, and then make them think again. But such effective rhetoric doesn't come out of a clear blue sky, it comes in a dense context, and here it's an intellectual one. In contrast, Hitler's famous rhetoric came in a political and historical context. Nazi ideology crumbled to dust in 1945 and those who had lived through its brief period of domination actually *couldn't say* what it had been when asked about it after the war, even though it had been strongly present throughout their schooling; there turned out simply *not to be* any intellectual context. But racism being *as bad as a plague* belongs firmly in the intellectual context of our new religion. It is the thing of all things that we must take seriously, the overwhelming moral concern; one might with extraordinary aptness liken it to the Black Death.

Questions of race aren't the whole of the new religion, but they reveal the creed's ideal and they lead straight to its centre which can be identified as 'social justice'. The whole movement of mind from 1945 to today is predicated on the idea of this justice and it has come to fill the gap left by orthodox belief. Like a religion it promises a better future for humanity and, indeed, a better present for individuals. A religion identifies clear enemies; for Protestants it was the Catholics, for the Sunni it is the Shia, for Muslims it can be 'the West', for Christians it was once Muslims, for certain Burmese Buddhists it has been the Muslim Rohingya, and so on – we know the pattern. In the new s-j religion the enemy is all those who might commit sins such as 'discrimination' or 'oppression' when these are directed at what used to be known as the Other. I suspect that the term 'the Other' has rather fallen out of use just because it seems to stress the otherness of other people; in fact it is simply code for 'that which is perceived as other', but it's easy to forget the qualification.

Social justice is also like a religion because it differentiates itself from the past. Protestants are (or were when they had any power) against the older Catholicism; communist believers had to exaggerate the crimes of the Tsars and the bourgeois capitalists to justify their violence; Christians quite quickly assumed a position of maximum hostility to the Jews and maintained it over many centuries. The new believers think that anything Conservative, or even conservative, is tarred with the brush of fascism, that any idea of tradition or the 'good old days' is false consciousness that will exclude the heretic from the communion of the faithful.

And social justice is like a religion because it offers an ideal, one not a million miles away from the promise in the Apocalypse that the lion will lie down with the lamb. One day, when we are all 'woke', the different races will be at peace and not abuse each other either in the smaller ways (verbal) or in the bigger ways (physical attack and social discrimination); women will not be abused in equivalent ways by words or actions that degrade them or disadvantage them; the poor will be given the same opportunities as the rich; exploitations of all kinds will cease and there will be no class advantages or social exclusions. So familiar is all this to us today that I hardly need to add further examples. The creed has been spelled out clearly enough and often enough and it is now the orthodoxy of Parliament, the BBC, all of education, the civil service, local government and so on. It is even the orthodoxy of the Christian churches where you are far more likely to get a mild socialist sermon on Sunday than you are to get anything about sin or hell or the blood of the lamb which will wash you (*je m'en excuse*) white.

Born in 1946 I feel in a good position to say that I have watched all this developing. The story of its inexorable rise is well told in Ed West's *Small Men on the Wrong Side of History* (2019) which is a personal narrative tracing the intellectual and social trends that have brought us all to believe, more or less, in this new religion, and he was born half a generation after me. What was a tendency among thinking and educated people to be more liberal, and in some case more socialist, in the 1960s has turned into an intolerant commitment to social justice at almost any price, something familiar to Christians whose history takes them from the gentle Jesus to the Inquisition, in slow time, admittedly, but with a certain inexorability.

One thing that made me think that we are dealing with a creed here, a belief system rather than just a political movement, was the strange realisation I had when the Me-Too movement got going in the wake of the Harvey Weinstein scandal. My first reaction, since I have a Quietist streak in me that dislikes demonstrations of all kinds and is suspicious when people start loudly claiming their 'rights' or proclaiming some 'identity', was to think that the women concerned were making too much fuss, that the matter could have been dealt with without this global tsunami of protest. But then I saw that the thing was not what I thought, for had I not been brought up ('I too' as it were) to treat women properly? Had I ever admired bullies, predators, rapists, gropers? Was I not, from my childhood in the now-derided 1950s onwards, strongly committed to decent behaviour towards women? Indeed, to good behaviour with anyone who seemed in any sense weaker than me, or disadvantaged in some way? Was I not known in my family as a person who had no difficulty making friends with foreigners? With women if you come to that.

So here were these women who were having to put up with the casting-couch jockeys, the Weinsteins and the Epsteins and presumably many other men with power. Horrible! Certainly not my idea of how to behave. And then what of my preferred recipe for change, which has always been gradual improvement and never revolution – a quiet word not a megaphone? Was that method still able to do the business in the modern world? I began to wonder.

Which is to say that when a new religion comes onto the field we, who may think we belong to an opposing army, will find as the campaign goes on and the other side gains more ground that some things do need to be rethought, even by their opponents. *Tempora mutantur et nos mutamur in illis* as they say.[19] And in the present case the religion of the woke has more or less swept the board.

Religions set up barriers that may not be crossed for ideological reasons. Victorian Christianity, scraps of which were still present when I was a boy, had it that one shouldn't swear and in particular that one should 'mind one's language' in front of the ladies and in matters religious. I remember my father correcting me when I was twelve or so after I had said 'Christ!' at some exacting moment of our domestic life. 'You mean *Crumbs*' he said sternly. And when I misunderstood the word 'orgasm' a little earlier in life it was my mother's turn. I wanted to be witty and accuse my brother, who was hogging the sugar one lunchtime, of 'having an orgy' with the bowl from which he was scooping the stuff. Alas, to make

---

19 'The times change and we change with them.'

it an even more exquisite sally I went further up the scale of what I took to be Decadent Party Code in English and came up with 'Stop having an orgasm with the brown sugar, bro.'[20] My mother was quite displeased.

Behold though. We advance to 2017 or so and we read about a politician who has lost her job for thoughtlessly using a word offensive to modern liberal thought. The context, where it was used as a weak clichéd expression rather than with any evil intention, seemed to most people to be only a minor offence. Common sense would probably suggest that the unthinking use of an old set phrase that happened to contain an unacceptable word would merit a rap over the knuckles, but the politician had crossed one of those lines that have been set up, in the same way as the lines of Victorians, to police language. No mercy was shown. It appears that some verbal sins cannot be forgiven any more in the new religion than they could be in the old.

The protestors who, around that same time, pulled down the statue of a seventeenth-century slave trader in Bristol and threw it into the harbour clearly felt that their religious beliefs about social justice meant that the normal rules about other peoples' property did not apply. Far worse, they also felt that they could crowd together in their protests and their destructive actions and not respect the 'social distancing' then in force, imposed in an effort to contain the coronavirus which by then had killed 40,000 people in the UK alone. The righteous anger of the religious mob transcends other socially-desirable norms which they, the protestors, may otherwise be strongly in

---

[20] This was English-boarding-school 'bro' of course, not a proleptic echo of American black culture.

favour of. Social justice, like religion for the believer, is more important than death.

We know that religious conviction can skew all thinking at times and here was an example: the potential death of their countrymen and women from Covid-19 was less important to these people in Bristol than a fairly trivial symbolic gesture against the statue of a long-deceased merchant. And of course that gesture is strangely reminiscent of the Protestant vandalism of English churches and monasteries under Henry VIII, which was done by those who believed as sincerely in their creed as any modern anti-racist. Indeed, both Catholic and Protestant 'martyrs' died in their hundreds in the sixteenth century merely for an idea (transubstantiation, say, or the language in which the Bible could be read) in a way of which I think the Saturday-afternoon indignants of today seem to be a weaker echo. The new beliefs are held with loud complaint but it's true that they have yet to produce much sacrifice or many saints.

Our new religion is, alas, an intolerant one which will 'no-platform' or silence dissent without much thought or debate. Modern conservatives on campuses and in churches today tend to feel like the Cathars in Béziers in the thirteenth century just before the Albigensian Crusade wiped them out – not in the right intellectual place for the times.

In thinking about all this from the perspective of the Enlightenment we come across a paradox. On the one hand the sort of left-liberal thinking that promotes an anti-racist and social-justice agenda is the clear heir of eighteenth-century rationalism, especially in its central concern with equality; on the other hand it is religiously-inclined to the silencing of other voices and to the intolerance of dissent or the discussion of 'wrong' ideas. And it was precisely such intolerance and arrogance that Voltaire and the others mounted their campaign against. These two inheritances provide the intellectual framework here: philosophically, do you prefer conservative/right/liberty (of speech for instance) or do you want socialist/left/equality (of different racial groups, of men and women and so on)?

The religion of science and the religion of social justice between them now leave little space for much else. Material life and material prosperity, along with this-worldly justice for all, have done to the older world (which is not that old; I am thinking of the 1950s) what Christianity did to the Roman Empire. Those who became Christians were no doubt many of them sincere, but reading Robin Lane-Fox and other historians[21] one gets a strong flavour of compromise and convenience in many of the conversions. More significantly from our point of view is the fact that the Roman state took control of education, for instance, which made it not only difficult to be a pagan any more but also made it difficult even to think pagan thoughts.

One is reminded of the ambitions of Stalin, Hitler, Mao, Pol Pot and the Kim dynasty in North Korea. Starve 'wrong' ideas of the opportunity to express themselves or be discussed and they will wither. If you accompany this with relentless propaganda in favour of the new ideas things will change pretty rapidly. Today we see that the commentariat and those paid by the government have quickly fallen into line – after all to some extent their jobs depend on it. Now, in spite of many years of Conservative government in the UK, the state has become enormous and its tentacles are

---

21 *Pagans and Christians: In the Mediterranean World from the Second Century AD to the Conversion of Constantine,* 2006

in some unexpected places such as the big charities whose budgets would not be half what they are if the government didn't quietly back them financially. The new establishment isn't Christian or communist or atheist or Muslim, but it has its religion and is working to convert us all. It believes in science and social justice.

Is it, incidentally, simply the religion of 'liberalism' that I'm talking about? The word 'liberal' resides in a famously vexed place. It can mean 'in support of a free market', 'in support of free speech' or 'in support of a range of ideas from feminism to the decriminalisation of drugs and gay rights'. It can refer to a supporter of the freedom to make money or to a supporter of no-platforming at universities, and its meanings vary according to country, most notably on the two sides of the Atlantic. But somewhere in there we can find the heart of our new secular religion. Essentially our new clergy of the left have abandoned the old notion of liberalism as individual freedom in favour of the newer (and more American) notion of liberalism as the freedom of the group.

Thus: the individual's freedom to smoke has been trumped by the group's right to be protected from cancer; the individual's right to teach his or her child about sex in their own way has been trumped by the requirement on schools to teach that homosexuality is normal; no individual is encouraged to set up a pernicious cult, one that disadvantages women for instance, but a *group* religion is allowed to flourish more or less unchecked that puts them well below men, encourages veiling and does not condemn FGM.

That this new group-mentality is in itself a religion is clear. The new orthodoxy is serious, censorious and intolerant, just like the old religions were. People in senior positions in government can lose their jobs and careers for merely saying a single unacceptable word. The feeling is that everything before the world 'woke' belongs to a time parallel to what in Islamic countries is known as the *Jahiliya*, the 'ignorance that existed before Mohammed' (its actions sometimes resemble the justification used by Muslim extremists for destroying the vestiges of pre-Islamic cultures, statues for example). Nothing good can be said about the British Empire, for instance, or about conservative values, without a sneer. The past was the domain of the 'stale, pale male' while the future is . . . well, we shall see.

The new religion is apocalyptic in that it looks forward to things getting better and better (the Whig interpretation of history) and it sees most past values as an enemy to be eradicated; it has a cavalier attitude (perhaps 'cavalier' isn't quite the right word here) to dissent and prefers the new-liberal value of being politically correct over the old-liberal value of free speech. It is bitterly opposed to other religions except where they are practised in a spirit of left-wing camp-following, as it appears many of them are, or where they are practised by non-Europeans – I think of Germaine Greer refusing to condemn FGM because she didn't want to bad-mouth Islam, and a quite sensible psychotherapist friend (female) who explained the advantages of veiling women to me, perfectly seriously.

Can we do better than this? Is there something we have missed? What of another, different kind of enlightenment? Where might it come from?

12. Consciousness is Enlightenment

Eckhart Tolle constantly repeats in his slow quiet voice that what we need is 'to be conscious'. By 'consciousness' he means subjectivity, awareness and above all the consciousness of consciousness, the awareness that we are aware. This self-reflexivity seems to be the extra layer that is particularly characteristic of humans. I wouldn't rule out categorically that those animals who are like us in some ways, perhaps chimpanzees who share ninety-eight per cent of human DNA, on some occasions can think about the fact that they are thinking; but this is a secondary question. The main thing here is that the most certain thing in the universe for us is that we are conscious beings and that we are able to be conscious of that fact. Everything else could be some sort of illusion or show, but we can't even start to ask whether the things we experience *are* illusions or shows without first accepting that 'we' are here doing the asking. As Galen Strawson says of conscious experience 'nothing in life is more certain'.[22]

Remembering this, and thus 'remembering ourselves', is the first step (and perhaps the last) in all enlightenment and it entails the Buddhist ideal of detachment. When we *step*

---

22 He doesn't mean 'Life is full of a number of certainties and this is the most certain of them.' He means 'Consciousness is the *only* certain thing we have.'

back and see that we are seeing, realise that we are thinking – and thinking that we are realising that we are thinking; we create a space in which we can see what is happening, be aware that it is happening here and now, and be aware that it's happening to *us*, to *me*. Whenever you hear Tolle suggesting that you be more conscious you do feel in that moment more aware of yourself and of the weight of experiencing – you sense the slight heft of it in your mind and your body.[23]

This is the enlightenment of the Buddha. We have a romantic notion that the Prince Shakayamuni sat under the Bodhi tree for a very long time and then something happened to him, suddenly and completely, in such a way that he rose a changed man and from then on was enlightened and had become the Buddha, permanently. Well, it may have happened like that, and it may have been a unique and perhaps divine moment, but for the rest of us things don't easily work in such an absolute fashion. For most people, and perhaps even for the prince himself who was a normal man after all, there are indeed moments of increased, enlightened consciousness and insight, but they alternate with more boring periods which themselves are interrupted by flashes and advances which then give way to retreats and setbacks, regroupings and other better and worse experiences. Nothing is permanent.

What is significant in the story however is not that it happened once, on that auspicious day in April 589 BC, but that it is always available to us, at least from time to time, if only we can remember to be conscious enough. I have never

---

23 Tolle's first and most famous book is self-explanatorily entitled *The Power of Now* (1997).

met anyone who claimed to be *permanently* wrapt in the *Samadhi* of infinite contemplation. Even the great Indian mystics and gurus of the last two hundred years such as Ramakrishna (I give a fairly recent example because modern biographies are less hagiographical than older ones) are often spoken of as 'falling into *Samadhi*' for a given period of time, sometimes longer and sometimes shorter; no claim is ever made that they are incessantly on another plane. So no, there are no permanent states here, we are in constant need of being re-enlightened. If we try for full consciousness as hard as we can it will turn out that, even if we feel we have made it for a few minutes, later that day we will probably imagine that we didn't really make it. We may also feel that we will never make it again.

But, like the Buddha, we can meditate. Meditation is the most direct way of trying to fix our consciousnesses – oddly, of course, because the focus of meditation is often on the mindless, on what the world would call 'nothing' but which the person meditating knows is not nothing. Meditation, which anyone can do, though it is true that some can do it more easily than others, changes our perspective and takes us some distance away from the world.[24] The interesting thing is the change in our consciousness that it produces, and twenty minutes a day will make a difference. Imagine then what happens in the Shaolin temple in China, for instance, where the winter retreat involves forty-nine consecutive days devoted entirely to meditation. The monks who participate go in shaven-headed as is the norm in Buddhist

---

24 A good recent book on the topic of meditation, and a sensible one, is Robert Wright's *Why Buddhism **Is** True*, of 2017. He apologises for the title which only came out like that because he wished to avoid repeating his surname. The bold letters are his.

monasteries and when they emerge they mostly have good heads of hair, which is something of a shock. But what has happened in there in the long dark days, besides hair-growth? One thing that most people can agree on, whether they are spiritually inclined or not, is that the minds of the monks have been affected. That at least will have happened, and it can be demonstrated in brain-scans. In other words their consciousnesses have a different flavour and their lives are now not the same as before. I imagine it is rather hard to interest them in the football scores or 'reality TV' when they come out blinking into the still-snowy courtyard.

And why should this be? Why should it be seen even by non-spiritual people as real and beneficial to devote time to focusing on Something Else, or on the Silence Within or on Nothing At All? What possible advantage can it gain us? Relaxation is available in other ways: clearing the mind can happen on a brisk walk in the woods; music can change our mood for the better. Is there some special enlightenment to be had in meditation? *Do* the monks emerge more enlightened as well as hairier? Could we do the same ourselves in a meditation class or even at home?

These questions are not only of interest in the area of self-help. If meditation can lower the blood-pressure or reduce stress nobody is going to be against it, of course, but what of the greater claims made for it? Are they just oriental exaggerations, the mumbo-jumbo of the spiritual East? We need to see the matter from the widest possible perspective. A change of perspective and an altered consciousness, *enlightenment* in fact, are not unique to Buddhist monasteries or modern meditation classes. There's a lot of it about everywhere. There are those who say that even *starting* to try to meditate is meditation. Perhaps we all do it on some level some of the time.

But what is it? In what way does it actually benefit us? What is its place in the great scheme of things? Let me present the dilemma which arises when we look at what modern research and investigation have revealed, which is not at all a simple material picture of the universe.

Theologians have been rightly criticised for proposing a 'God of the gaps' who arises wherever science leaves space for Him (or Her). In this scenario God had a picture of how He wanted human history to go – until Marx filled that gap. Then God separately created each of the species found in nature – until Darwin shut that down. And then God was deeply involved in our personal lives – until Freud revealed the workings of the unconscious. As the gaps closed God retreated and became thinner, more abstract, further driven into corners. But simultaneously the ever-increasing body of evidence that there is some other force or entity in the cosmos which may be the explanation of paranormal phenomena, near-death experiences, mediumship, telepathy and so on, not to mention the mere existence of gravity, electricity, quantum effects, black holes and dark energy, began to demand proper consideration. 'Spirituality' began to take up some of the space vacated by 'God' and it can now be seen as central rather than peripheral.

But this tendency has still much work to do and a balancing act is needed. It is rather obvious to those who are open to the spiritual that we can change tack to the benefit of all, but putting the boat about isn't easy. Science, rather than 'God', can account for most things, up to a point, and leaving 'Him' in the empty gaps between the explanations smacks of desperation. But, instead, there is the likelihood that there exists some exceptional and unexplained energy that may partially account for the mysteries still left by science (black holes, consciousness) and also for all the things left outside the gates of science such as NDEs, precognitive visions, end-of-life experiences and so on. We need science but we also need to give some account of the myriad phenomena of the 'unscientific' in the universe.

Thus: meditation 'works' not just because it slows down our physical brains and helps us relax but because it alters our auras, the energy bodies that surround us. You can get an aura camera to show this[25] and you can demonstrate telepathy with simple experiments.[26] Mediums do sometimes tune into something which gives them accurate information about dead people, information that can be verified. People do have precognitive visions of events in the future.[27] Poltergeists are rare but real.[28] The evidence, which should be getting thinner and thinner as science finds alternative explanations, has in fact become quite a lot more solid in recent decades.[29]

Now all this may be erroneous or the result of some grand misunderstanding about what is going on. Perhaps we are the victims of a really huge international hoax. But these

---

25 The Dalai Lama, when filmed in meditation, looks all right on the screen for the first few minutes and then disappears as he goes into his trance. The screen remains grey for forty minutes or so and then he emerges from the trance and the camera shows him again, sitting there as before (cf. Victor Chan, *The Wisdom of Compassion*, 2012).

26 See Rupert Sheldrake, many publications, and Guy Lyon Playfair, *Twin Telepathy*, 2012.

27 See Ann Treherne, *Arthur and Me*, available on Amazon, 2020.

28 See David Fontana, *Is There an Afterlife?*, 2005

29 On NDEs for instance see Raymond Moody, *Life After Life*, 1975; also Pin Van Lommel, *Consciousness Beyond Life*, 2004, and a hundred books in between.

explanations (error, fraud, hoax, radical misunderstanding) look less and less likely as time goes on and, *prima facie*, it looks as if my short list of phenomena includes enough evidence for it to be at least considered seriously. So let us just do the thought-experiment of accepting that the millions of NDEs and the hundreds of thousands of successful mediumistic connections and all the other paranormal phenomena seen on the planet are, provisionally, sometimes in some way real. Then a great deal falls into place.

When we seem to be 'getting' something in our meditations, and feel it to be something outside our heads, perhaps we really are tuning in to some other level of reality. When people have NDEs perhaps we don't need to scrabble around seeking an explanation in the unlikely area of oxygen-deprivation. Perhaps precognitive visions come from some place that is not amenable to ordinary science. Perhaps twins who have clear telepathic connections aren't lying about them. Perhaps healers really are connecting to something like the 'spirits' who they say are helping them. Perhaps there is a 'spirit' dimension in the universe generally. Perhaps some elements of 'magic' and mind-reading and some elements of psychic detective work depend on the same energy, force, dimension or level that all my other examples also possess or rely on. Perhaps, as some mediums say, our 'normal' world is only separated from this alternative dimension by something as thin as a sheet of paper. It would explain a lot of otherwise inexplicable phenomena.

In order not to frighten the horses I think we could profitably improve our vocabulary in this area. The most important thing is to play down the dualism ('heaven and earth', 'the other side') and try to think of the 'spiritual' world as being intertwined with the 'natural' world rather than in opposition to it.[30] Talk of 'the supernatural' doesn't help credibility and offends common sense and, although it is convenient to use the word 'spirit', it might be best to realise that it too is some sort of metaphor. 'Spirit' could be left aside where we can speak instead about 'an unexplained energy' or 'a subtle energy' that co-exists with the known (but also unexplained) energies of the universe: gravity, electro-magnetism and the strong and weak nuclear forces. For clearly the hot hands of the healer and, *a fortiori*, the success of healers who work with animals,[31] along with the sense that mediums get that some force is presenting ideas, feelings and names to their minds, and the communications achieved in telepathy, along with many other such phenomena, add up to an energy field which is worth exploring and which surely is not best described, lazily, as just 'other-worldly'.

This energy field can be shown on an aura camera and felt during meditation. Its force may help to account, negatively, for the drop in temperature often experienced by those contacting the dead. It could be at the origin of healing effects and those other planet-wide effects described by Dean Radin in his two main books. *The Conscious Universe*, 1998 and *Entangled Minds*, 2006. And, of course, we may touch it lightly in our more successful moments of meditation.

Let's look ahead, in another thought-experiment, to the intellectual future, the likely thought-paradigms of the

---

30 Rupert Sheldrake, on YouTube in 2020, asks that we stop calling certain events 'paranormal' or 'parapsychological' because, as he says, 'they are normal.'
31 John McManaway, the healer from Fife, can demonstrate that he is paid real money by Scottish farmers to cure their valuable bulls. No greater proof of his efficacy could be given.

twenty-second century. The religion of science will not have given up; on the contrary it will surely still be flourishing. But increasing globalisation, which has already opened people's minds to the spiritual insights of other cultures and traditions, will continue and our identities will become increasingly flexible and selective. There is already no social pressure at all, in Europe at least, that is likely to forbid any given person, young or old, from declaring him or herself an atheist, a Buddhist, a pagan, a born-again Christian, a Muslim or a believer in *Star Trek*. Perhaps the religion of social justice, with its clearly Christian roots, will be taken to a higher level as it replaces the older religions in the West, but it has few metaphysical presuppositions. The central plank of its platform, equality in all its forms, will mean that now that the protection and encouragement of the *body* has been established (no more slavery, women no longer tied to the kitchen sink or to incessant childbirth for instance), and the protection and political correction of the *mind* has been promulgated (no more patriarchal religion, no more obligation to believe or practise anything), the third element in our present trilogy will get its turn: the *spirit* will claim its rightful place.

In this light I should like to finish with our place in the cosmos. Once again, who are we? Who am I? These questions seem to have shifted slightly and, at their deepest level, to be susceptible of an answer of a surprisingly simple kind.

Throughout the history of Western thought there has been an obstinate problem. It is a at the level of deep ontology and deep epistemology and it can be felt in the series of major dichotomies known as *idealism vs realism, mind vs matter, spirit vs flesh, consciousness vs the physical brain*, and so on. The Abrahamic religions tackled it, so did Plato and Aristotle; Descartes did his best, as would Kant and Hegel; science has tried its hand and post-structuralism has tried to dodge round the question rather niftily. I could prolong this narrative to a great extent, but the important thing here is to state simply and clearly that this problem, the 'mind–body problem', *has not been solved*. Many clever things have been said about it but most of them either propose slightly unlikely solutions or merely express the problem with greater clarity. In the first category must come Descartes himself with his reliance on a gland in the head (the pineal gland) to do the work of marrying mind and matter, bringing together what he called *res cogitans* and *res extensa*. In the second category (a clearer expression of the question) comes Wittgenstein's nice restatement of the problem when he asks us to imagine a very, very small person strolling around in the brain. This nano-human would see all sorts of things including the brain apparently 'working', but he would never, ever see a thought. For modern philosophers, led by the Australian philosopher David Chalmers, the question of consciousness is simply 'the hard question'.

But there is another theme in philosophy, recently revived, that seems to deal fairly well with this difficulty. Some mainstream thinkers have entertained it and written rather well on it though it remains somewhat the Cinderella of philosophy, derided or ignored and *underfunded* as we would now say. And yet it is a new, quite penetrating idea that is presenting itself in our philosophical arenas which suggests that a way forward as we continue to bump our heads again and again on the hard problem. It is an idea with the apparently barely-serious name of *panpsychism*. The advantage that this theory has is that it can (a) deal with some of the questions left aside by the mainstream thinking of the Enlightenment (questions at the materialist or mechanical level such as 'What happened just before the Big Bang?') and (b) it can open a space for the possibility of enlightenment in the other sense, the experiential reality of consciousness (and its concomitant probability, the spiritual), the area of life which, whatever you may think of it, hasn't gone away and is looking a little bit stronger with every decade that passes (besides being, by common consent, the only thing we actually know for sure).

Panpsychism objects to the arbitrary division of nature into two (say, mind and body) and proposes that, since it's quite hard to make everything a 'machine' on the one hand and a little odd to insist on everything being purely mental on the other, the answer might lie in some as-yet-undefined conjunction of the two. In an earlier essay I wrote of the dimensions of spirit and matter being like the two sides of a piece of paper.

The history of philosophy is littered with the detritus of this debate. Plotinus with his passionate defence of all sorts of spiritual dimensions 'above' our own is at one extreme of the long battleground, and at the other end is the atheist Sartre who, to make any sense at all of the disenchanted world of modernity, proposes bluntly that there are two sorts of thing in the universe, namely things and our ideas about things. Only the most violently hard-nosed physicalists will want to turn thought, subjectivity and *qualia* literally into brute matter[32] and, as we see, even Sartre cannot do it. So

---

32 This is the thesis of the respected elder statesman of American philosophy Daniel Dennett who claims to believe that thoughts actually are the electrochemical impulses in our brains. In spite of the respect in which Dennett is held Galen Strawson has found only one way to describe this sort of thinking: '*silliness*'.

we need a newer, simpler picture that, without claiming to explain the universe, can at least put this old tug-of-war to bed. It can be sketched as follows.

There are two aspects of any analysis of anything: the external, measurable, scientific aspect (revealed to us by the Galileo–Bacon-Hobbes–Descartes programme and the Enlightenment) and the internal, subjective, experiential aspect that is not amenable to science as presently constituted, that we call 'consciousness' and that is revealed in its greatest clarity in Buddhist notions of enlightenment and perhaps also in paranormal and spiritual phenomena. Between them they make up the universe.

Panpsychism suggests that it is unimaginable that subjectivity and consciousness simply sprang from gas, rocks and mud with nothing proto-mental to precede them. The 'internal' *must always have been there* even if only to accord with the logical requirement for there to be something in each cause that permits us to see the connection between that cause and its effect. If an effect is evident, room must be made for a cause. Thus somehow, unimaginably, our minds must belong to a dimension or part of the universe (although it has somehow to be present in the whole of it) that is the same age as and co-extensive with the 'material' universe.

There is no mind–body problem then. How it happens I cannot say, but the fact must be that everything physical is, as Teilhard de Chardin put it, 'lined with thought'. Even the rocks. This apparent absurdity looks a little less absurd when we remember that in the Enlightenment there were philosophers who seriously suggested that dogs were incapable of feeling pain as they were only machines – whereas we humans were something higher. This separation between us and nature has had some highly dangerous consequences, for the planet and thus for us. But things seem to be changing: nowadays we are increasingly aware of the sensitivities not only of animals but also of plants, of forests and of the less obviously 'en-minded' elements in nature. We are, inexorably, on our way to 'en-minding' rocks, electrons and *quanta*.

We do not have an explanation of this or even any very good map of what it might look like, but all philosophers dislike the miraculous and it is generally considered that the emergence of thought and subjectivity from utterly different, non-minded, inert, absolutely non-subjective substances is nothing short of an impossible miracle.[33] But the 'absurdity' of rocks lined with thought is, if you think about it, slightly less of a miracle than the one involved in something emerging, against the most basic of all the laws of logic and nature (*ex nihilo nihil fit*), from nothing.

I end then with an image of a more united universe, for surely there can't be any radical ontological split between different parts of the one cosmos. And even if such an idea is too much to swallow yet-awhile let us agree on this, which is pretty much uncontroversial: we do not know what things are 'in themselves'; the irreducible *quanta* keep their secrets well hidden; Kant tells us that we can know *phenomena* but not *noumena*, things in *themselves*. Even Bertrand Russell, no airy speculator, opined that that we know 'nothing' of 'the intrinsic nature of an electron'. Science is very good at telling us the 'how' but less good at telling us the 'what'.

---

33 See David Skrbina, *Panpsychism in the West*, 2nd edn, 2017, and Philip Goff, *Galileo's Error*, 2017.

So it is not the case that the 'common-sense materialism' of our mainstream thinking today, grandchild of the Enlightenment, has all the answers. On the contrary it comes up short and hard when it meets the *intrinsic* nature of things-in-general, about which it ultimately knows nothing, and harder when bumping against the intrinsic nature of 'material' things (which are, after all, more like packets of energy than they are like 'things') than it does when trying to get a grip on immaterial, mental, subjective things.

The last step for Enlightenment thinking, then, having come so far and so fast with such spectacular results, is to see that the things it cannot deal with may need another turn of the intellectual wheel, one which demands an openness to a new sort of thinking that for the moment I will call 'spiritual'. By that I mean, first of all, a thinking in which the energy that is the underpinning of material science may be a mirror image of the energy that we feel inside us as conscious minds and subjects. This is the energy that we have glimpses of in the near-death experience, in meditation and in many 'psi' phenomena, and it will help explain the plethora of 'paranormal' events with which the world, as we now know, is quite literally filled.

The Renaissance and the Enlightenment did an extraordinary job, but in their scientific successes they emphasised the mathematical, the measurable and the material too exclusively and made what Philip Goff calls 'Galileo's Error',[34] plunging further and further into the objective measurement of nature and ignoring the subjective, the experiential and the conscious. Their effect was to change our world view from that of the Christian

---

34 Philip Goff, *Galileo's Error*.

centuries ('The mechanistic worldview once liberated humanity from religious dogma')[35] and this has been very useful indeed. As we have seen in some of these essays it has not been an achievement without costs (overpopulation, destruction of the environment, atomic weapons), but it has nonetheless stood us, on the whole, in good stead and it is the great gift Europe has given to the world.

'Now it appears to have outlived its usefulness.'[36] Any new world view is going to have to accommodate nature in a less exploitative and consumerist way and to admit the experiential and subjective into its metaphysics not as an optional supplement but as a recognition of things always-already present in the picture. The word to take us to the place where we will stand a chance of making this change is 'enlightenment' with the Buddhist small initial letter. The enlightened ones of the earth, Buddhist or not, seem automatically to have had a better attitude towards nature than has been normal in the last five centuries. St Francis of Assisi talking to the animals, presented to me in my Catholic childhood as a holy but essentially eccentric figure, may be the kind of hero we need to adopt rather than the violent, political, economically-obsessed leaders who have led us to ever-greater prosperity and ever-greater misery, uprootedness, alienation and danger for the future. St Francis thought that the birds he spoke to had some kind of mind, or 'soul' as he would have called it, and that can be taken as an emblem of a new more modest view of ourselves in which we share *all nature with all nature*: atoms, cells, minerals, plants and animals. This sharing cannot only be

---

35 David Skrbina, *Panpsychism in the West*, p. 333.
36 David Skrbina, *Panpsychism in the West*, p. 333.

a matter of machines – we know it can't because our lives are actually spent not in the material but in the mental and because there is a mental dimension that is the one thing widely regarded by philosophers as certain; indeed it is the only thing we each individually know for certain, as even Descartes admitted. This dimension, our mental, conscious nature, as much as the physical nature which we share with all of the rest of nature, is before us. We need only to open our enlightened minds to see it, indeed to *be* it.